T0361734

THE UNTOLD STORY OF SCOTT HOYING, PENTATONIX STAR

THE UNTOLD STORY OF SCOTT HOYING, PENTATONIX STAR

My Son's Journey to Find Harmony in Music and Life

CONNIE HOYING

With help from
LINDSAY HOYING FONDREN

Foreword by
SCOTT HOYING

ROWMAN & LITTLEFIELD
Lanham • Boulder • New York • London

Rowman & Littlefield
Bloomsbury Publishing Inc, 1385 Broadway, New York, NY 10018, USA
Bloomsbury Publishing Plc, 50 Bedford Square, London, WC1B 3DP, UK
Bloomsbury Publishing Ireland, 29 Earlsfort Terrace, Dublin 2, D02 AY28, Ireland
www.rowman.com

British Library Cataloguing in Publication Information Available

Library of Congress Cataloging-in-Publication Data

Names: Hoying, Connie, author. | Hoying, Scott, 1991- writer of foreword.
Title: The untold story of Scott Hoying, Pentatonix star : my son's journey to find harmony in music and life / Connie Hoying ; with help from Lindsay Hoying Fondren ; foreword by Scott Hoying.
Description: Lanham, Maryland : Rowman & Littlefield, 2025. | Includes index.
Identifiers: LCCN 2024044431 (print) | LCCN 2024044432 (ebook) | ISBN 9798881804930 (cloth) | ISBN 9798881804947 (ebook)
Subjects: LCSH: Hoying, Scott, 1991- | Hoying, Scott, 1991—Family. | Hoying, Scott, 1991—Childhood and youth. | Hoying, Connie. | Singers—United States— Biography. | Gay musicians—United States—Biography. | Pentatonix (Vocal group)
Classification: LCC ML420.H74 H69 2025 (print) | LCC ML420.H74 (ebook) | DDC 782.42164092 [B]—dc23/eng/20240920
LC record available at https://lccn.loc.gov/2024044431
LC ebook record available at https://lccn.loc.gov/2024044432

For product safety related questions contact productsafety@bloomsbury.com.

♾™ The paper used in this publication meets the minimum requirements of American National Standard for Information Sciences—Permanence of Paper for Printed Library Materials, ANSI/NISO Z39.48-1992

To Rick, Lindsay, Lauren, and Scott. I love you all so much. You have been my biggest cheerleaders and my most honest critics throughout this process. I appreciate everything you have done to help make this dream a reality. Thank you for making life so interesting.

Contents

CONTENTS

Online Supplement

This book contains online supplemental media, courtesy of the author and the Hoying family. Visit the website below to discover videos, songs, and other related materials:

www.conniehoying.com/bonuscontent

A musical note symbol ♪ in this book will mark every instance of corresponding online supplemental material.

FOREWORD

Scott Hoying

I've realized that "success" is a very complicated word. It can mean different things to different people. For some, it might be getting a master's degree and a great job. For others, it may be creating the next huge app or buying a fancy car. Or becoming a pop star. Or moving out of their hometown.

My idea of success has been ever-changing throughout my life. Currently, I think of it more as a *feeling* rather than a *destination*. As of today, my definition of "success" is *a feeling of gratitude to have built a life in which you consistently feel content, high in self-esteem, and fulfilled.*

Whether you're spending time with loved ones, working, or playing—that moment you think, *Wow! I feel like a kid again and so lucky to be in this place* is success to me. How much money you make, how many people like you, how many number ones on the charts you have ≠ sustained happiness. One of my favorite quotes ever is from Jim Carrey: "I think everybody should get rich and famous and do everything they ever dreamed of so they can see that it's not the answer."

I love this quote because I've found that the beloved dopamine spike you get from money and fame is very temporary. The brain has a funny way of adapting. When Pentatonix was first taking off, I genuinely can't even explain how joyous and viscerally thrilling it felt. *Wow!* I was on top of the world!

Then I realized I would have to keep working harder than ever to sustain that. So I did. But my brain kept adapting. I increasingly put pressure on myself to keep that thrilling high going, and I got stuck on the hamster wheel. I slowly started to let anxiety and cloudy intentions rule my creative and personal decisions, got lost in the opinions of others, and for a moment, forgot what my true passions even were. So I took some shortcuts to dopamine and probably drank more than I should.

For a moment there, I may have been seen as successful, but I was in a pretty dark place. Fortunately, I'm back and doing better than ever. I learned some life-changing, valuable lessons along the way—one of which is that contentment, self-esteem, and fulfillment come from within. I also learned that all of us may already have everything we need to start experiencing success right now.

Some people have "succeeded" but aren't happy. Some have succeeded but don't even realize it yet.

Again, it's different for everyone, but I personally feel most successful when I *lean into* my deepest passions and relationships. (Having enough money is important, too, but only because it removes stressors and aids in bringing about freedom—resulting in gratitude and contentment.)

I say all this because I think the number one thing that led me personally to success was my home and family life. When I was a kid, I was very lucky to have a home of love, safety, and unconditional support. My parents encouraged my sisters and me to follow any and all of our dreams, however big or small. It was always like this.

To this day, I know I have a home where I'm welcome and safe. Growing up, I never even thought about financial success. My dad and I were playing video games. My mom was setting up the karaoke machine. My sister Lauren and I were belting out "Hero" by Mariah Carey. My sister Lindsay and I were making DIY horror movies, like *The Bloody Hand Killer* on an old VHS camcorder (Oscar-worthy, to be honest!). It was a creative, happy place for the most part.

I didn't envy the kids who had more than I did because, one, I didn't process that I was supposed to, and two, I didn't have any interest in those things. I loved my exact reality. Without a doubt, that was one of the most impactful factors that led me personally to success. (There are infinite routes to success that look very different, but here is mine!)

My homelife made the world a little less scary and helped me cultivate resilience—an essential skill that played a major role in leading me to where I am now in my home, work, and love life. Resilience can be cultivated in so many different ways, and I honestly believe it isn't talked about enough. I have faced rejection countless times—and still do to this day. That, unfortunately, doesn't go away.

However, my parents didn't seem too worried about it as I was growing up. When *American Idol*, *X-Factor*, *America's Got Talent*, and *The Voice* all said "No! No! No! No! No! No! No!" (cue "Bohemian Rhapsody") sometimes paired with "You just don't have what it takes!" my parents would calmly say afterward, "Ah! Their loss! Who cares what they think?" or "They're wrong. Such a bummer, but you're so amazing and you crushed it!" or even "Let's learn from this and keep going. Moving on!"

Although I didn't know it at the time, I was internalizing, *Oh, my worth doesn't have to come from how well these things go!*— that failure does not define me. Each moment of rejection was simply an opportunity to grow. Thus I have never really connected failure to my personal worth. Every up and down of life has been worth it and has taught me valuable things. This caused a butterfly effect.

Resilience led to the courage to take risks. Taking risks led to pushing boundaries and braving unknowns. Which led to progress, growth, purpose, self-esteem, and hope—which led to a sense of purpose and fulfillment. Which then led to the ultimate: sweet, sweet gratitude. *Success!*

But it all started with unconditional love: the love my mom showed me, the love my dad showed me, and the love my sisters showed me.

Unconditional Love → Resilience → Fearlessness → Risk
Taking → Purpose → Self-Esteem → Attraction → Gratitude
(*Success!*)

Now I am beginning to build my own wonderful life with my
beautiful husband, Mark. We hope to pass down these values
to our future children: that they always will have a safe place to
land; that they can be brave, follow their dreams, and *lean into* life
without fear of failure.

———

It's been such a beautiful experience watching my mom write
this book. She absolutely loved every second of the process. She's
spent so much time interviewing people, writing, rewriting, and
doing research. Her passion is infectious and inspiring. That's
success! She has already succeeded because she's cultivated an
environment and headspace where she feels motivated to fear-
lessly spend hours passionately writing about her children whom
she loves endlessly.

As you read this book—the ups, downs, wins, losses, joys,
struggles—I encourage you to notice the through line of love and
support and the butterfly effect they cause over time. Whether
you're pursuing your dreams, raising a child with big dreams,
or simply curious about the untold story of that tall dude from
Pentatonix, I hope this book leaves you inspired and motivated
to *lean into* life and love and pursue your passions, however big or
small. (My mom tends to have that effect on people.) You'd be
surprised what wonderful things it can attract into your life!

———

Love you, Mom! Go get 'em!

PREFACE

As a mother, witnessing your child achieve their dreams is one of life's greatest joys.

From being that toddler in the day care center whose mouth was taped shut for singing too much to touring the world with the Grammy-winning a cappella group Pentatonix and living his best life with husband Mark, my son Scott Hoying has had a remarkable journey.

Scott's passion for music was unmistakable even at a young age. His dedication and creativity set him apart, sending him on a path to extraordinary success. His road to stardom was filled with moments of triumph and adversity, enduring support, and relentless pursuit of excellence.

This book delves into Scott's story, highlighting the values, principles, and pivotal moments that shaped the way his musical career and life evolved. It's a reflection on nurturing talent, resilience, and the impact of a supportive family. My husband and I are proud to have raised three incredibly successful children, each with their own unique paths. For parents, educators, and aspiring artists, this book offers insights and inspiration from Scott's experiences.

Welcome to Scott's story.

Welcome to our story.

———

Over the years I have often been approached by people posing several questions: What did we do to help Scott achieve his dream of having a successful music career? What is the secret to raising three successful children? Then there's the million-dollar question: Who is the musician in the family, Rick or me? Occasionally, people suggested I offer classes, give talks, or even write a book regarding the above questions. So I've taken up the challenge. The bulk of this work discusses Scott's musical journey, including the rise of Pentatonix, peppered with some parenting insights I've learned as a mother of three children. I also provide a glimpse into our family's musical heritage.

I discuss Scott's decision to come out to me as gay at the age of seventeen. This was a pivotal moment in his life, filled with both heavy emotions and personal challenges as well as significant accomplishments. It was also the beginning of my journey to fully understand and accept his true self. Through love, open conversations, and steadfast support, I embraced his identity and stood by him as he pursued his dreams, aware of the challenges I knew he would face. "Coming out" as a teenager is often fraught with difficulties, and for Scott, this experience was intensified by his aspirations to pursue a career in the public eye. I dive into the challenges Scott and many LGBTQ+ teens encounter: fear of rejection, bullying, and the pressure to conform to societal norms.

Initially, I never thought I could write a book about Scott and our life in general, and I'm not sure why I've decided to do it now. Maybe Scott, with all his creative energy, inspires me to do things I wouldn't normally think I could do. Maybe it's because I'm retired, and I have the time. But I think it is deeper than that. When Scott got married, in July 2023, I felt like it was the end of an era, the closing of a chapter. Our last child, "the baby" of the family, was now married. It made me think of what a life we'd had up to that point and that is when, for the first time, I thought to myself, *Maybe I will write a book.* Raising three children over thirty years, the ups and downs, the challenges, Scott's musical journey, all the adventures—these might be interesting to people, and it would be a detailed journal for our family. Whatever the case, I'm happy I decided to take on this project.

Through the process, I've reconnected with numerous individuals who played a significant role in Scott's musical upbringing, and I've gained new insights into the musical heritage of my family. There are striking parallels between Scott's musical talents and those of his grandmother and even his great-great-grandmother, Grandma Bottens. Grandma Bottens's life story has even inspired the story of yet another project for Scott.

———

We always encouraged our children to explore a variety of activities. In their early years, we chose activities for them with a broader purpose in mind: to nurture their mind, body, and soul. When they were young, I made them all take up swimming and soccer. Lindsay and Lauren participated in dance. Ironically, Scott didn't take dance, but it turns out he has become an incredible dancer!

That covered the "body" part. For the "mind," along with school and reading every day, we played board games and brain games and always asked them questions, making them think about things. Church activities and music gave them a foundation for their "souls."

As they grew older, they chose activities that interested them. For Scott, our youngest child (six and eight years younger than his sisters), it was a blend of music and basketball, with music eventually taking center stage. He also loved video games and, as is the case with many folks nowadays, probably spent a little too much time absorbed in these digital worlds.

Lauren, our middle child, found her calling in music and volleyball. During high school, volleyball took precedence, even helping her lead her high school team to the final four state championships two years in a row and make the Junior Olympic VB team. She still pursued singing whenever possible. Today she's thriving as the lead singer of a band, performing gigs regularly. Lauren also had a passion for airplanes, like her dad. She has worked at Lockheed Martin for sixteen years in aeronautics, and because of her, we get VIP treatment at airshows all over.

Lindsay, our oldest, on the other hand, developed a love for learning and languages at a very young age. I remember her obsessing about Spanish class in kindergarten, and she became fluent in German as an exchange student during her junior year of high school. Growing up, she learned several instruments, played volleyball, and did photography, but languages stuck with her. She joined the US Navy after college and has spent her career traveling the world as a linguist, learning several languages and dialects. She currently teaches at the Defense Language Institute for the Navy and has added several more degrees in the process. Lindsay has been stationed all over the world, giving us the opportunity to visit her in these amazing and interesting places. On the side, she still does photography and videography.

———

I believe it's important to let your child discover their own paths. Not everyone in our family tree was afforded such freedom until much later in life. Rick and I, probably like most parents, had no idea what we were doing in the beginning. In hindsight, giving them that freedom was the most important thing we did. We never tried to force any of our kids into what we wanted them to be. We are not perfect and we made mistakes, but we loved them, accepted them for who they were, and supported them in pursuing their goals however we could. We worked hard to provide them opportunities, and it allowed our kids to develop and hone their talents.

While I revisited old notes and calendars accumulated over the years and pored over pictures and videos to help me reconstruct Scott's journey, I couldn't help but think of that little boy with blond hair and blue eyes who captivated the family with heartfelt renditions of songs from *The Lion King* at the age of just two.

During the writing of this book, I had conversations with his friends, choir directors, vocal coaches, piano teachers, recording engineers, record producers, and many of the people involved with Pentatonix over the last thirteen years, which revealed a wealth of untold stories. I was reminded of many moments that had long been forgotten. I was able to hear anecdotes, behind-the-scenes stories, and unique insights—some of which were new to me—that provided an even deeper understanding of Scott's life up to the age of thirty. While it was challenging to find detailed records for some years, I've striven to piece together as complete a narrative as I could. These conversations became a treasure trove of memories, causing a flood of emotions. The rekindling of these memories makes Rick and I all the more proud of what Scott and his sisters have accomplished.

At nineteen years old, Scott found himself catapulted into the beginnings of a career he had long pursued. However, his journey toward this pivotal moment didn't commence in his teens. From a young age, Scott dedicated himself tirelessly to his passion for music.

By the time Pentatonix began to rise, Scott had already amassed a wealth of experience and expertise, setting a solid foundation for the extraordinary career that awaited him. All these years of effort have come to fruition at his (still) young age. His story serves as a testament to the power of persistence and the rewards of pursuing one's dreams from early on. It's also a story of community and living life as your most authentic and true self.

You'll explore Scott's personal experiences, the obstacles he encountered, and how he overcame them. You'll also share in the lessons he's learned along the way and how his attitude played a role in his achievements. He is a fountain of optimism!

———

Scott lives by two quotes:

What would you do if you knew you could not fail?

I believe that is why he never hesitates to start another new project. And

When one door closes, another one will open.

That is why rejections never slowed him down, and I suspect they never will.

CHAPTER 1

From One Generation to Another

Nick Lachey was onstage, and he paused before announcing the winner of *The Sing-Off*. The air was thick, and the audience was at the edge of their seats. During what felt like an eternity, all I could think was, *They have to win.*

Scott had worked so hard for this most of his life, and if Nick didn't announce Pentatonix as the winner, I might have had a meltdown. This moment felt like the culmination of so many years of dreams, hard work, and unstoppable determination. I couldn't help but think back to when Scott was just four years old, standing in our living room, as he declared he wanted to sing for people all over the world to make them happy. That innocent statement was the beginning of an incredible journey that has taken us through countless piano lessons, voice lessons, choir practices, auditions, and late-night rehearsals.

Sitting in the audience, I felt an overwhelming sense of gratitude for every moment, every note sung, and every obstacle overcome. This moment was more than just the announcement of a winner—it was the validation of Scott's lifelong passion.

———

We knew from an early age that Scott was blessed with a musical gift. He has a combination of genetic predisposition, skills gained from long hours of practice, and an intense passion that began when he was very young. Music always came naturally to him, and considering our family's musical past, it's not all that surprising.

Scott's great-great-grandmother was Sylvia Lincoln-Lasswell-Rose-Bottens, though I always knew her as Grandma Bottens because she was with her third husband, Henry Bottens, by the time I was born. And what a history this grandma has–buckle up!

Throughout the years, it was said that we were related to Abraham Lincoln, the connection tracing back to Great-Grandma Botten's grandfather, Eli Lincoln. This was a source of fascination for our family. In grade school, when the teacher would ask, "What is an interesting fact about you?", I was always quick to say, "I'm related to Abe Lincoln." However, as more ancestry sites have come out regarding genealogy, my sister, Kathy, did a deep dive. She couldn't find the exact connection, but she did discover that Eli's family and Abe's family originated from the same place in England and later lived near each other in Illinois. I have a picture of Eli, and the resemblance to Abraham Lincoln is striking. With his tall stature, distinctive facial features, and similar eyes, Eli looks like Abe's twin. So until proven otherwise, I'm choosing to believe we are related.

Grandma Bottens may not have been a president, but she was definitely interesting in her own right. She defied the social norms of her era and was a rebel back in the early 1900s. My mom used to tell me that Grandma Bottens was the epitome of a "women's libber" and loved that she went to protests, fighting for a woman's right to vote. Her three marriages were pretty scandalous for the time. Most women seldom got divorced once, let alone multiple times in the early 1900s.

More importantly, Grandma Bottens had a passion for jazz music and a talent on the piano, despite being unable to read music (she strictly played by ear). She also had a grit or gumption that led her to put together a jazz band. Her band included two of my mom's uncles, Jack and Joe, and they traveled all over the United States with Grandma Bottens as their pianist, entertaining audiences in dives, saloons, and other venues. Even though she was never famous, I like to think of her as one of the many groundbreaking women who helped pave the way for today's female musicians or anyone who deviated from musical norms.

After her second divorce, she packed her bags and brought her seven-year-old son (my grandfather) with her onto a train to New Mexico. There she decided to stay put for a bit to give him some semblance of a normal life, and she earned a living playing piano at a local saloon to earn money. While this wasn't exactly the most common lifestyle for a woman back then, she still did well enough to support them. By the time she married her third husband, she had moved back to Iowa, where she continued to play the piano in local venues.

Grandma Bottens lived with us in her later years, and I remember her giving piano lessons to my older sister, Barb, while I sat nearby and watched. When each lesson was over, they would play and sing Grandma Botten's favorite song, "Red Sails in the Sunset," a classic written by Hugh Williams. Afterward, she would treat us to chocolate chip cookies and milk and tell us stories of the "good ol' days." I was very young at the time, but I loved listening to her talk about her adventures. She would talk about the Roaring Twenties, Prohibition (although Grandma said most people got around it, and she was very familiar with "speakeasy" establishments), women's suffrage, and of course, her days of playing the piano in saloons. When Barb and I recently were talking about Grandma Bottens for the book, we both laughed when Barb said, "She remembered some wild stories she used to tell us."

Grandma Bottens had many talents and passions. In her later years, she made beautiful quilts—one she called "Grandma's Flower Garden," which Barb displays in her home. Barb must have inherited her quilting skills, because she has made dozens of them over the years. She also loved playing checkers, a game she taught us with patience. It seems a bit unfair that we each inherited different aspects of her obsessions: Scott with her love for music, Barb with her quilting skills, and me with her chocolate chip cookie obsession (although I can play a pretty mean game of checkers—just ask my grandsons). It's a small but sweet connection to her.

Even though I was young when she passed away, Grandma Bottens made a lasting impression on Barb and me. One night, Barb told me that she was out with her friends, and they were going to a movie. All of a sudden, she heard someone call out her name. It sounded like Grandma Bottens's voice. When she turned around, no one was there. She had a bad feeling and wanted to go home, but her friends talked her out of it. Sadly, that night Grandma Bottens passed away.

I had six siblings in total, including Barb, and out of all of us, Barb was the closest to Grandma Bottens. She was devastated and really felt like Grandma Bottens was saying goodbye to her that night. I may not remember all the stories, but I do remember Grandma Bottens being sweet and also a little spicy. I would learn later, she was especially spicy, even a bit feisty, in her younger years as a jazz musician, unafraid of walking her own path, her way.

———

Scott's grandmother (my mother, Arlene Lasswell Hoenig) also deeply loved music from a young age, and her extraordinary talent did not go unnoticed. When she graduated from high school in 1942, she was offered a scholarship to a music school in Chicago—an opportunity that could have changed the direction of her life. Despite growing up with a musical mother, my

Figure 1.1 Great-Grandma Bottens and her band, Melody Kings. Author's family photo.

grandfather refused to let her go. My mother believed his decision may have been influenced by his own tumultuous upbringing, marked by constant travel and multiple stepdads. Regardless of her potential and talent, my mother wasn't allowed to attend college in Chicago to study music; instead, she stayed in her hometown of Fort Madison, Iowa.

Not long after that, my mother married my dad. She stayed home, raised seven children, and became a foster parent to several more. As a child, I remember my mom singing beautiful power ballads like "Somewhere over the Rainbow" while she did chores around the house. Her voice was very powerful and would fill our home with warmth. In church, she was often a featured soloist, singing moving renditions of hymns like "How Great Thou Art" and "The Lord's Prayer." She also played piano by ear only and wrote a book of poems/songs. She had a musical passion that lived within her and continued to inspire her until her dying day.

My dad shared a musical interest with her. He loved to sing and would often belt out hymns at church. However, unlike her, he was tone-deaf and blissfully unaware of it. His enthusiastic singing was loud and off-key, and while part of me wanted to ask him to stop, I never did, because it was clear how much joy it brought him. Despite her amazing voice, my mom never said a word or even gave him a funny look. It must have driven her crazy, but she never let it show. Perhaps she saw the joy, too, and it trumped his distance from the actual pitch.

———

On many occasions, I've found myself seated in an audience, captivated by the songs sung by Scott or my daughter, Lauren, who is also musical, whether it's a ballad or the national anthem. In those moments, nostalgia washes over me, thinking about my mother's own strong voice. I can't help but connect her musical talent to theirs. I miss her, and sometimes I am also sad for her, wondering what her life would have been like if she had taken a different path. Of course, that path might not have included me, which means Lindsay, Lauren, and Scott would not be here either. I shudder to think about that scenario and the music the world would have never experienced.

Despite motherhood and family responsibilities, music was still a part of my mother's life. She continued singing at churches around Iowa, Illinois, and Missouri and starred in local musicals. But my grandfather's refusal to let her attend college in Chicago wasn't the end of her college dreams. At fifty-two, after my siblings and I were grown, she pursued her deferred dream and enrolled in college to study music. In 1981, almost forty years after her first opportunity to study music in college, she graduated with a degree in music.

I was so proud of her. She could have easily left life as it was; she already had a life she could be proud of. Her perseverance was

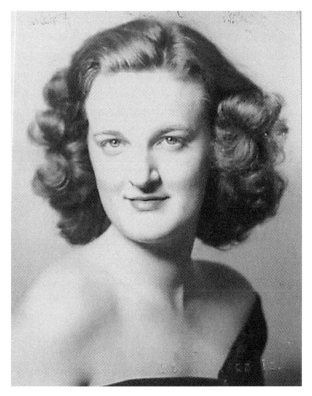

Figure 1.2 My mother in her younger years. Author's family photo.

a testament to her lifelong love of music and a lesson for me: You can follow your dreams and passions at any time.

Her tenacity and our family legacy of music and independence is a thread throughout generations of my family. But, whether through coincidence or something else, the musical inclination seems to skip every other generation. I played clarinet in high school and was in a few musicals (no lead roles). But that is about as far as I went with music until the COVID-19 pandemic, when I took an online piano course at home. I enjoyed that class immensely, but it's nothing compared to the devotion and undeniable talents of Grandma Bottens, my mom, or Scott.

My husband Rick has always had a passion for music too. I love hearing him play guitar and sing, and I am still in awe of his creativity and ability to express himself through music. He had no formal training but still wrote songs, taught himself to play guitar, and sang most of his life. When Rick and I were dating, he would come over to my apartment, play his guitar, and sing. I'm pretty sure that's part of why I fell in love with him.

Rick and I met at a bar called The Slope, in Winter Park, Colorado. I was engaged at the time but was having doubts about the upcoming wedding. I fell head over heels for Rick and quickly broke it off with my fiancé. It reminds me a little of Grandma Bottens, maybe, but I wasn't married yet.

My first date with Rick was a Kenny Loggins concert at the iconic Red Rocks in Denver. In 2013, we had a full-circle moment when Pentatonix opened for Kenny Loggins at South by Southwest in Austin. After the concert, I had the privilege of meeting the legendary artist, thanks to Scott, and was able to share our memories of him during that unforgettable night in Denver. I knew from the beginning that Rick was it for me, and over forty years later, I am still so in love (and a fan of Kenny Loggins).

Rick wrote many songs in his twenties, and little did he know that two of them would reappear forty years later. For Rick's sixtieth birthday, Scott wanted to do something really special. Scott found two songs on an old cassette tape of Rick's: One was a tribute to his own mother, "Praise of a Good Woman," and the other was about ladies playing games, "Games" (this was before we met). In secret, Scott decided to rerecord both original songs, keeping Rick's vocals, adding his own, and turning both songs into duets.

When Rick's sixtieth birthday came around, our family and friends got together to celebrate the milestone. As the evening unfolded, Scott stood up and asked everyone to listen for a moment. With a smile, he announced the surprise: two new recordings of Rick's old songs, now reimagined with both

Figure 1.3 Rick and his guitar. Author's family photo.

of their voices. Hearing Scott's voice blend with his own from so many years ago is hard to describe. It was overwhelming for Rick—really, for all of us—to hear the old crackling tape and my husband's voice from forty years before, combined with my son's, likely around the same age. It was as if the past and present had

9

Figure 1.4 Rick and I met Kenny Loggins thirty years after our first date going to his concert. Author's family photo.

come together at that moment. My husband says that birthday party was one of the most touching moments of his life, not just celebrating his sixty years, but demonstrating the powerful bond between father and son. ♪

Rick also wrote songs about events in our life. I still think about the song Rick wrote when our oldest daughter, Lindsay, was born. That was a scary time. After a complicated labor, she was born blue and not breathing. We thought we had lost her. But after six days in the NICU, we finally brought her home. Before I even got home from the hospital, Rick had written a beautiful song.

As our family grew, Rick continued to weave music and creativity into our everyday lives. Rick would sing bedtime songs to our children and was particularly effective at lulling them to sleep. These were not your everyday bedtime songs but unique, original songs every time. He would make songs up on the spot that were tailored to each child. The lyrics were about them or summarized the day or talked about upcoming events. These are some of my favorite memories of those early years.

One time, Lindsay and Lauren were fighting and whining at me to settle their argument. I was getting very frustrated with the situation, and all I could think to do was to tell them that if they didn't work it out, Dad wouldn't sing to them that night. Surprisingly, it worked, and they immediately came to an agreement. I'm not sure threats are the best parenting approach, but sometimes you gotta get creative.

———

Scott's musical influences in our home extended beyond Rick. He was also inspired by his sisters, Lindsay on the piano or one of her other instruments and Lauren singing around the house and at various places around the Dallas/Fort Worth area. When Scott arrived, music surrounded him in our home, and he immediately joined in. He learned to appreciate different instruments, various music genres, and varied vocal styles. Musical talent and a shared love of music connected Scott and his sisters early on. Between the three of them, the sound of singing, piano, guitar, violin, and for a bit, even oboe, saxophone, and bassoon were ever-present around the house. Every week, at least one of the kids had another recital, concert, or other music-related activity.

During the early years, we bought a karaoke machine, which quickly became a favorite, complete with frequent impromptu karaoke nights. It became almost a daily ritual, with Scott and Lauren enthusiastically belting out songs. Rick also captured just about everything we did through video, so I can still go back and relive a toddler Scott and an eight-year-old Lauren pouring their hearts into each performance. One of our favorites was Lauren

Figure 1.5 Rick and Scott at the piano. Author's family photo.

singing Anne Murray's "Something' to Talk About," which is one of the first songs Scott remembers. He told me recently that she did it so well that it made him want to sing.

However, the center of Scott's early musical world wasn't a single person; it was a thing: the piano. We had a piano in our music room, and he was constantly there. As a two-year-old, Scott would sit at the piano and bang on the keys, but even then, he looked like a concert pianist, his hands moving up and down the length of the piano. As he got older, he would play simple replications of what his sisters played, trying to imitate their melodies. Recognizing his innate talent, we knew we had to nurture it. We worked hard and, fortunately, were able to provide Scott

Figure 1.6   Scott and Lauren at the piano. Author's family photo.

with the right setting and tools. We made sure he had lessons and the space to develop his skills with some fantastic local piano and voice teachers. The mentorship Scott received from these teachers was invaluable. They pushed him to challenge himself, explore different genres, and develop his unique sound.

Our support went beyond the practical, though; we were his biggest cheerleaders, attending every performance, celebrating his successes, and encouraging him through each challenge. A child's potential can be nurtured and developed with the right support, encouragement, and dedication. They can achieve whatever they can imagine.

Scott had so much behind him, urging him on, in addition to generations of musical involvement and interest, and maybe some genetics all the way back to at least Grandma Bottens. My mom, sadly, passed away just before Pentatonix was on *The Sing-Off*. After she and my dad moved to Texas, they would go to every show or recital the kids were in. She would have loved watching her grandson perform in front of a television audience, sharing his talent on such a big stage. As a kid, he had big dreams, and I wonder if she knew they would one day become real.

CHAPTER 2

Texas Bound

"Bloom where you're planted." This is a saying that my father-in-law, Tony, has repeated many times over the years, and it was an important part of our family's philosophy. Change is an inevitable part of life, and sometimes it can be daunting. Whether switching careers, moving to a new city, or simply embracing personal growth, we experience difficult moments when we face uncertainty and still have to push forward.

Moving, in particular, is an exciting but stressful life change that most people will go through at least a couple of times in their lives. It can be hard to picture what your new life will look like, and that unknown can be scary. Rick was somewhat used to it, since his family of seven moved multiple times throughout his childhood..

Before Scott came along, Rick and I were living near the foothills of the Rocky Mountains, just outside Golden, Colorado. The view from our backyard was, to say the least, stunning. We were a young family with a toddler (Lindsay) and a newborn (Lauren). Rick worked for Pizza Hut in real estate, and I was a physical therapist at a nearby hospital in Arvada. Though we had no family nearby, we were surrounded by many friends and enjoyed a busy and fun-filled existence. Everything seemed perfect, but a huge change was just around the corner.

In January 1986, Lauren was just a few days old, and Rick was still home in the middle of his paternity leave when he got a call from his boss. He told Rick he needed to talk in person and that he should come to the office immediately.

Rick had never received a call like this before, so he nervously left right away while I waited at home, fearing the worst. When Rick got to the office, his boss sat him down and told him the news. They were closing the Denver office, and he could no longer work there. Fortunately, he told Rick that he could keep his job if he transferred to Dallas, Texas. Rick asked for some time to talk with me before making a decision.

This was an incredibly difficult decision since Golden, Colorado, had been our home since we were married and where we had met in 1981. We loved skiing in the mountains and were apprehensive about leaving it all behind for some hot southern state we had never been to that was known for cowboy hats and horses.

We didn't know anyone in Texas at the time, and it sounded almost like a foreign country to me. It did spark a sense of excitement and possibilities, though, and the thought of staying behind and looking for a new job was not appealing to Rick. We agreed to the transfer to Texas and started planning our move.

Fortunately, the move was fairly easy. Pizza Hut bought our home in Colorado and paid for the move. The moving company packed everything except the bare essentials we would need until we moved into a new house. A few months later, we were on our way, with our lively two-year-old, Lindsay, and our colicky three-month-old, Lauren, in tow.

———

Those early days in Texas became a busy chapter in our family story. There was so much to do: finding a home, a church, a doctor, a new job for me, day care for the girls, a racquetball club, meeting new people, and a thousand other things. Being strangers in Texas, we had our work cut out for us.

While looking for a home, I was really focused on finding a good school system even though our girls weren't school age yet. After careful consideration and quite a bit of searching, we found what we were looking for. We bought a house in Arlington, a smaller city (at the time) situated between Dallas and Fort Worth. It was close enough to the city where Rick's new office would be, but it also seemed like a good place to raise children. The neighborhood not only offered the promise of an excellent school district but also had a sense of community that made us feel right at home. In our new neighborhood, there were plenty of children around the same age as ours as well as older teenagers who eventually became our go-to babysitters.

The school district we chose had an excellent reputation in academics but also in extracurricular activities. We were not especially aware then, but the district also had incredible music programs. From elementary through high school, the focus on music education was extraordinary. Over the next several years, we put our kids in every activity known to humankind, including soccer, swimming, baseball, softball, basketball, and, yes, music. The kids sang in choirs, took piano, were in musical theater, and learned to play several instruments. As they grew, they started to narrow their activities down to the ones they liked the most. It wasn't easy at times, especially when all three children had to be in three different places simultaneously. It seemed we ate most of our meals in the car after stopping at drive-through restaurants. To us, it was a necessity, because we firmly believed the kids needed to experience as much as they could and find what they loved.

———

I wasn't sure at times I could manage it all. And Scott wasn't even born yet. It started to feel overwhelming when Lauren was four and Lindsay was six. One day, amid the chaos of their typical sibling antics and with Rick being out of town, I felt especially desperate—I thought I might be losing my sanity. They were good kids, but like any children, they sometimes argued and whined, pushing each other's and my buttons. The following day, I stumbled upon an advertisement in the newspaper for a lecture by a child developmental expert named Kevin Leman. He wrote a book called *Making Children Mind without Losing Yours*. It felt like a sign, so I signed up for the lecture, bought the book, and read it in a single day. After a quick reread, I began implementing his parenting strategies, which started yielding results almost instantly. With his coaching, I found ways to encourage better attitudes and positive behavior and, most importantly, to get my kids to talk to me, which worked rather well. They still call me all the time to tell me everything going on in their lives.

In one example, the girls were arguing and trying to drag me into it. Remembering advice from Leman's book—to separate them from the parents—I put them in the backyard. I told them to work it out and then they could come back in. Well, I didn't realize the June bugs were out in full force, and they were everywhere. The girls started crying, pounding on the door, saying they had worked it out. I don't recommend scaring your kids with June bugs, but separating them from you and pushing them to settle their arguments on their own can be very effective. And really, they were going to have to get used to June bugs living in Texas!

Another lesson learned from Leman's book had to do with accountability. Scott learned a hard lesson when he was about five. While at a gas station with Rick, Scott stole a bag of Skittles after being refused candy. After discovering the theft, Rick wanted to make sure he knew that stealing was unacceptable. He drove back to the gas station and made Scott return the half-eaten bag and apologize to the gas station attendant. Scott says this is a core memory and that he's never stolen again.

———

Attending Leman's lecture was the icing on the cake. Meeting him in person, getting my book signed, and expressing my gratitude for his help (and my sanity) felt like a small victory. His chuckle and humble acknowledgment warmed my heart, and he assured me that he was glad he could make a difference.

That book became my parenting bible, a well-worn guide I revisited countless times while raising my children. I also explored his book *The Birth Order Book*, which was a fascinating exploration of how birth order within a family significantly influences a child's personality. It offered valuable insight and became another cornerstone in our parenting approach. I can't help but credit Leman's books for helping mold my three children. They were well-behaved kids who went on to become successful adults, and I'm not sure how I would have done it without Leman. Here are just a few of the topics he addresses:

- Get your kids to talk to you (anyone who knows me knows my kids talk to me quite frequently, even as adults).
- The seven principles of reality discipline (highly recommended)
  1. Establish a healthy authority over your children.
  2. Hold your children accountable. (No free Skittles, as Scott knows.)
  3. Let reality be the teacher.
  4. Let your actions match your words.
  5. Stick to your guns, but don't shoot yourself in the foot.
  6. Relationships come before rules and activities.
  7. Live by your values.
- Rear responsible adults who are difference makers in the world (we achieved this with all three of our kids).

For any parents navigating the joys and challenges of raising young children, I wholeheartedly recommend Leman's library of books for tips and insights to bring out the best in your little ones.

CHAPTER 3

Scott Arrives

Scott was born on September 17, 1991, at Arlington Memorial Hospital in Texas. He was delivered via C-section, scheduled for me due to the difficult births of his sisters. As the only one born in Texas, Scott is the only true native Texan in our family. We were overjoyed to have a son, but we hadn't agreed on a name yet, so he went home from the hospital without one. One name we considered was Leo Anthony, in honor of both of his grandfathers. To this day, I regret not choosing that name. I thought it sounded old-fashioned and worried that he might not like it when he got older.

However, I couldn't have been more wrong. Scott loves the name Leo and even considered using it as his stage name when he left for college. Lindsay wanted him to be named Louis because she thought all three of them should have names that began with an L, but we weren't too keen on that one. Leo could have worked for everyone if I hadn't focused on future "what-ifs."

While I was still in the hospital, a friend came to visit me. We were discussing names, and he mentioned that if he could rename his son, he would name him Scott. When I asked why, he responded, "Because it's a good name for an athlete." This really resonated with me because Rick and I had both played sports our entire lives. We were still playing softball (I even briefly played in college) and racquetball up until Scott was born. So I thought there might be a possibility that our children could be pretty athletic. Believe it or not, a musician's name wasn't on our radar, despite our family history. Years later, when I told Scott this story, he gave me a "Seriously, Mom, you've got to be kidding." Sorry, Scott. I suppose it could have been worse. At least I didn't name him after Yogi Berra!

After leaving the hospital with our unnamed baby boy, the name Scott kept resonating with me, and I thought his middle name could be Richard, after his dad. Ultimately, we decided on Scott Richard Hoying.

I always took a few months off from work after having a baby. I had done that with both girls and had planned to take off a bit longer with Scott, now having three children. However, when he

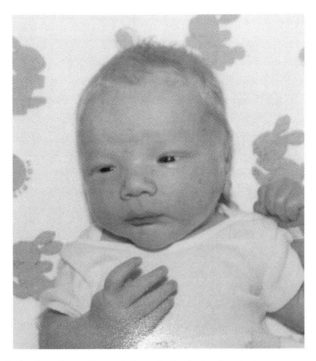

Figure 3.1 Scott's newborn picture. Author's family photo.

was just four months old, I started to feel restless, a bit depressed even. I was confused by these feelings because, after two daughters, I was thrilled to be a mom again, and to finally have a son, and I had never experienced a similar restlessness before. How could I feel this way when I had everything I ever wanted in my life at that point? Though I felt lost and unsure how to cope with these emotions, the thought of telling a therapist that my life was wonderful and fulfilling but I felt depressed seemed impossible. In retrospect, I believe I was suffering from postpartum depression, which wasn't a subject that was discussed as much back in those days.

Thank goodness, mental health is being talked about more these days, so other mothers might be more likely to seek out help. So much more is known about postpartum depression today, and health-care providers now have a range of effective treatment options. More women can receive the care and support they need during this challenging time and avoid the sadness I felt.

As a self-imposed treatment, I decided to go back to work part-time and still be home by the time the girls got home from school. I hoped that working again would resolve this unexplained sadness or at least distract me from it. I always enjoyed being a physical therapist, and it was an incredibly rewarding job. I slowly started to feel better, and being around friends and coworkers again also helped. I eventually felt like my normal self again.

I was fortunate that returning to work seemed to help my issue. I never told anyone about my struggles, not even Rick. I felt embarrassed or worried it might scare him when, really, I was hardly alone in struggling after the birth of a baby.

Scott was five months old by the time I had everything in place to return to work. I had found a home day care for Scott. A friend recommended a young mom named Jennifer, who had an infant around the same age as Scott. She wanted to stay home with her baby but needed a little extra money. Jennifer had a delightful and bubbly personality, making her exactly the type of person I would feel comfortable leaving Scott with, and she came highly recommended.

She often commented on how much music seemed to impact Scott's mood. After babysitting him for about a month, she told me that if she turned off the music playing on the radio, he would have a full-on meltdown! As soon as she turned it back on, he would immediately stop crying, and once again, he would be happy and content. We had already begun to notice Scott's eyes lighting up when he heard singing or songs on the radio, and he would sway and wriggle along. Since music was always playing in our house one way or another, he was a happy baby most of the time. The music that filled our home reflected my preferences— Elton John, Doobie Brothers, or the Eagles—as well as those Rick loved, like Charlie Daniels and Jim Croce. Scott grew up listening to these songs, and as he got older, he would often play and sing them. Scott even did a cover of "Long Train Runnin'," by the Doobie Brothers, on his first album.

———

At age two, Scott became obsessed with a show called *Barney &* *Friends*. The lovable purple dinosaur and all those catchy tunes were another early influence and a surefire way to lift his spirits. Around the house, we would all sing and dance along to "I Love You, You Love Me" and "Clean Up, Clean Up." The latter proved especially useful over the years. I was thankful the show included a song to encourage cleanliness. If you've seen a house with three young kids, you understand.

Scott mastered picking up clothes for the most part, but the habit of picking up towels never quite stuck. Even now, when he's home, he leaves wet towels on the floor and grabs a new one every day, which drives me crazy! I guess even the power of Barney has its limits.

As a toddler, no matter where Scott was or what he was doing, if I called out, "Scott, Barney is on," he would run to the living room and plop himself down in front of the TV, soon completely absorbed in the world of that purple dinosaur. He would dance and sing along without a care in the world. For years, he even carried a purple Barney dinosaur wherever he went. When Barney sang, "I love you," I knew Scott loved him too.

Once he was in kindergarten, Scott seemed to lose interest in the show and suddenly stopped carrying Barney around. I assumed it was because he outgrew his purple dinosaur phase. But I found out later that when he had taken his Barney to school for show-and-tell, some kids had made fun of him. He put Barney on a shelf in his room, and that's where it stayed for years. I was surprised kids could be that mean at such a young age. I guess bullying has no age requirement. I am so glad that a few years later, Scott would have a chance to reclaim and own his early love of Barney with an appearance on the show!

Jennifer took care of Scott until he turned three, when she decided to return to work full-time. I wanted to keep working part-time and we felt Scott was ready to attend a day care facility. Conveniently, a brand-new facility had just opened up a block

Figure 3.2 Scott, Barney, and Lauren. Author's family photo.

from our house, so we decided to enroll him there. I was a little nervous. We had grown so comfortable with him being at a home day care for so long, and it had been almost five years since we had a child in a day care center. For some reason, I had anxious, intrusive thoughts about his safety. Maybe many parents do. It's hard to deal with that worry, though it's understandable. And people may even tell new mothers to relax and calm down. But our vigilance can also help keep our babies safe.

In December 1994, I found out that I had every reason to worry. Scott had only attended the day care center for a few months when I received a distressing phone call from the mother of one of Scott's day care friends. She informed me that her son had told her that Scott's mouth was taped shut and he had been placed in a closet while at school. I couldn't believe what I was hearing. I was horrified and so angry I was shaking. I dropped my keys three times on the way out the door, and it was all I could do to focus and drive. The mama bear in me had been released. Upon reaching the day care, I made a beeline for the director's office and unleashed my barrage of questions: Why on earth would a member of your staff tape my three-year-old son's mouth shut and put him in a closet? Do you endorse such behavior? What is wrong with your staff? And why was I not notified?

When my rant was over, the director disclosed that the guilty party was the teacher's aide. She claimed it was because Scott would not stop singing in class, and she lost her temper.

I shouted, "He is three years old! What was he disturbing, coloring hour?" The director told me that his regular teacher had stepped out of the room briefly, and when she returned, she noticed Scott was not in the room. She asked where he was, and Scott's classmates yelled, "In the closet!"

The teacher immediately got him out and removed the tape. The director assured me that the teacher's aide had been promptly dismissed and escorted off the premises. While I appreciated the immediate action taken, I still felt the need to withdraw Scott from that day care immediately. I couldn't trust them and knew I would never feel comfortable with him there. Why hadn't they called me first? Why was I just hearing about this secondhand from another child's mother? Scott and I gathered his belongings and left.

On the way home in the car, I turned to Scott and asked why he hadn't told me what had happened the day before. He said he didn't want to get into trouble. I almost cried. I told him that he could always tell me things, good or bad, and what the teacher's aide did was wrong. Scott, with a sense of relief, said, "She wasn't there today." I told Scott that she would not be teaching there anymore and that we were going to search for a new school.

He simply replied, "OK."

Despite his simple response, it was not OK. This incident left a lasting impression on me, reforming my approach to Scott's education and care. I became much more vigilant about making sure there was appropriate supervision before I'd let Scott go anywhere. Scott still remembers being in that closet to this day in vivid detail. He said being physically silenced for singing is one of his very first memories.

There was a silver lining in all of this, however. We enrolled him at a new day care, Children's University, which was not far away, and had a very different experience there. His new teacher had a music degree and was happy about Scott's continuous singing. He recognized Scott's talent and encouraged him. He was amazed that Scott could sing perfectly on key and in rhythm, which was remarkable for a three-year-old. The teacher suggested that Scott start learning to play the piano and emphasized the importance of encouraging his musical talents early. That teacher worked with Scott as much as he could, teaching him songs, beats, rhythms, and notes. There's no doubt he helped foster his love of music, raising him up, rather than pushing him down, in the process.

—•—

Lauren loved singing, too, which played a huge part in Scott's musical development, especially in group singing. When Lauren was ten years old, she became friends with a girl named Courtney, who also sang. It just so happened that Courtney's father, Larry Tardy, was the music minister at a local church and introduced us to Marlene Bigley. Marlene had just moved to Texas from California, where she specialized in preparing kids for auditions like Disney, commercials, *Star Search*, and more. Marlene started TKO Kids and TKO Tots in Texas as a way to remedy the lack of platforms that showcased talented children and their performance abilities. The two groups sang all over the United States, including the state capital, the Alamo, the White House, fairs, and malls. They did holiday programs, too, like Christmas and Fourth of July shows.

When Lauren joined TKO Kids, Marlene had just decided to create another group, TKO Tots, for younger kids. They were often siblings of the TKO Kids. At age four, Scott was thrilled to join the Tots and eagerly learned the songs and simple choreography. He was a natural performer and loved being in front of an audience. This is where he really started getting noticed for his talent.

Around the same time, Rick learned from a friend he played guitar with at church about the musical duo Trout Fishing in America, Keith Grimwood and Ezra Idlet. His friend mentioned that the duo was performing at Caravan of Dreams in Fort Worth and suggested that our kids might enjoy it. Unfortunately, our daughters were busy with other activities, so Rick took Scott alone.

Rick said afterward that Scott was mesmerized and never took his eyes off the performers the entire concert. This was when Scott decided 100 percent what he wanted to do with his life. Scott came home and immediately told me that he wanted to sing for people all over the world and make them happy, just as that concert had done for him. From that day onward, Scott's passion

Figure 3.3 TKO Tots. Paul Knudson

for music grew with purpose. He had a goal, and nothing could stop him.

Trout Fishing in America's music basically became the soundtrack of our lives. Our girls ended up loving them, too, and we all quickly memorized many of their songs. Whether we were setting out on a long road trip or just hanging out at home, their songs were always there. Their lyrics are clever and fun for kids and adults alike.

Eventually, Scott and Rick became a kind of unofficial cover band for Trout Fishing, with Rick on guitar and Scott belting out the songs. They performed at church talent shows, senior facilities, and schools. "Day Care Blues" was a big favorite along with "18 Wheels on a Big Rig," "My Hair Had a Party Last Night," "Pico de Gallo," and "Nobody." Anywhere they performed, they were a hit.

We attended every Trout Fishing in America concert we could, always making sure to be there whenever they performed at a nearby venue. Even to this day, when we get together for the holidays or a family reunion, we find ourselves randomly singing "Pico de Gallo" or "Need a Bandaid": "Pico de gallo, you oughta give it a try-o."

———◆———

Rick was always an active member of our church choir. At age five, Scott expressed his wish to sing with his dad in the choir. Years later, Scott told me that part of the reason he wanted to be in the choir was that he was really bored and had trouble sitting still. He said he needed to channel his energy into something. Initially, I had some reservations, worried that the adults in the group might not be enthusiastic about having such a young child join them. However, any doubts I had quickly disappeared. The choir members welcomed him with open arms, and Scott learned so much from them. They even commented on how he would harmonize with them during the songs. They were amazed that he did this naturally without any practice at only five years old.

Having noticed this ability in the car with songs on the radio, we weren't surprised by his abilities at church. Rick once asked Scott if he knew what harmony was, and he quickly responded, "Yes, Dad, my teacher taught me about it. Isn't it cool?" Indeed, it was.

Before singing in the church choir, Scott would stand near and emulate the choir director, mirroring every movement with

Figure 3.4 Scott and Ezra—from Trout Fishing in America—in Kerrville, Texas. Author's family photo.

his arms. Everyone seemed to enjoy it, so we let him continue doing it. It's fascinating watching Scott at a Pentatonix concert, guiding the audience in a song for a TikTok post. He moves like a choral director while teaching them their parts, just like he did as a kid.

As Scott grew older, he began to perform solos within the choir. On one occasion, Scott sang "I Can Only Imagine" by the band Mercy Me. The powerful rendition earned him a standing ovation, which probably wasn't entirely expected or appropriate for our church. A guest priest even mildly reprimanded the congregation, explaining that songs in church are not so much performances as they are prayers. The church secretary pulled me aside the following week at church and told me they had received several calls that week complaining about the guest priest's comments. Scott continued to sing at our church throughout high school and remained an integral part of the choir. Even when Scott moved to California and started his career with Pentatonix, he would regularly return as a guest soloist at Christmas Eve and Easter masses. Among our cherished memories are his duets with Lauren, particularly in arrangements of "Oh Holy Night" and "Mary, Did You Know?"

I'll never forget the time Scott sang "Hallelujah" with Christmas lyrics that Pentatonix had written. They had planned to release this rendition of the song, but Leonard Cohen and his camp decided at the last minute they weren't comfortable having it released with the new lyrics. It turned out OK because their cover of the original can be listened to all year long and is one of their most watched videos on YouTube. At this writing, it has been viewed 748 million times. The song achieved significant success on several *Billboard* charts, including reaching number one on the *Billboard* Hot Christian Songs, placing number two on the *Billboard* Digital Songs, number two on Holiday 100 (even without changing to the Christmas lyrics), and peaking at number twenty-three on the *Billboard* Hot 100 chart.

As Scott gained fame, we had to start attending Christmas-morning mass. Otherwise, we would have been up too late, waiting for Scott to finish taking selfies with fans after the midnight mass on Christmas Eve, sometimes until 2:00 or 3:00 a.m. One thing about Scott is he never, ever says no to a fan who asks for a selfie. He doesn't ever want to seem like he isn't grateful for their support, even when he needs his sleep to open presents on Christmas morning.

Fun Fact: The "Mary, Did You Know?" arrangement was crafted with Lauren's assistance. Years later, Pentatonix performed this very arrangement, which has amassed over three hundred million views on YouTube.

———

While cassette tapes were still a thing, Lauren had left some practice tapes in the car. Among them was a recording of "Unchained Melody," which she was preparing to sing at a show. Having heard Lauren sing it so many times, he pressed play and began to sing it himself, confidently tackling even the challenging high parts. I remember being stunned that he could sing it that well. Eventually, that song became a regular in his repertoire.

But it wasn't just songs that Scott collected. He was still fascinated by the piano, with a growing interest in what a keyboard could do. We already had an electric piano for several years. It was versatile, allowing the layering of beats, and featured a built-in metronome and sound effects. The kids were able to test out different rhythms, beats, and instrument sounds, as well as many music genres. Scott and his sisters spent hours on that piano, and it inspired all kinds of new creativity.

If Scott wasn't watching his sisters play, he would be on the piano himself, creating his own musical arrangements with the different built-in accompaniments. Often, he would sit down after the girls were done playing and play their songs by ear. He would try different keys and manage to figure out simple versions of what they played. Even back then, I started to wonder where this would all lead.

When Scott was five, we decided it was finally time to enroll Scott in piano lessons. He was more than ready. He started with Keli Ferrier, who had taught Lindsay and Lauren for several years. She had already done an excellent job with the girls and was excited to start with Scott. Lindsay and Lauren had shared stories of Scott's love of music, and Keli had met Scott before in passing. They became fast friends, and their enthusiasm as teacher and student was evident. Scott was finally getting formal music lessons, and he committed himself wholeheartedly.

Keli quickly recognized that Scott was no ordinary student. With every lesson, he progressed rapidly, and after a few weeks of lessons, Keli told me after a lesson, "Scott is a prodigy. I've never taught anyone like him." Following each lesson, I would ask him

Figure 3.5　Keli, piano teacher, and the kids. Author's family photo.

what his favorite thing he learned that day was. He consistently cited musical elements like notes, dynamics, or articulations. Still, like many youngsters taking piano lessons, he would rather play songs than practice scales, including "Für Elise," one of my favorites. I understood. "But scales are important," I explained. He responded with, "I guess," and shrugged his shoulders. ♪

I didn't just ask Scott what he learned at piano lessons. I would ask him and his sisters about their school day activities, trying to gauge their homework load. I was also interested, of course, and happy when they described each class in detail. I believe this habit is why all three of my kids still call me regularly, even in their thirties and forties, to share updates about their lives. *A simple question does a lot.*

As piano lessons progressed, I noticed Scott would breeze through his lesson books in just one or two weeks. He was obsessed with the piano and would wake up early, even before the sun was up, to practice. When Scott got home from school, his backpack would hardly hit the floor before he was back at the piano, soon lost for hours in a world of music.

I often found myself fielding questions from other parents about how I got Scott to practice. Many had heard him perform during talent shows and were curious how I might have encouraged his evident devotion when they had difficulty getting their son or daughter to practice. Was there a trick? I really didn't know what to say because I *never* had to encourage him to practice. In fact, I had to tell him to *stop* so he could do his homework or eat dinner! But thinking back, if Scott loved a song like "Für Elise" or the "Jurassic Park" theme song, he would be glued to the piano until he mastered it. I wish I had realized then that finding songs kids love is a great way to encourage them to practice. One time, I told a mom that I thought it was the type of electric piano we had that made it fun to practice, but she looked at me like I was crazy. Another mom came to our house one day to drop something off, and Scott happened to be playing. With a serious expression, she placed her hand on my shoulder and said, "Don't ever let him quit." I assured her I didn't think he would ever *want* to quit. I remember it so vividly because, behind her words, I heard genuine emotion. I wondered who in her life had given up on music too soon. Perhaps it was she.

To this day, whenever Scott comes home for a visit, he gravitates to the piano. He plays and sings songs he's working on. When Scott was working on his first musical, he treated us to a preview of songs he was writing. The emotion in his performance moved me to tears. As he had been early on, he was wholly inside the music. Maybe I didn't have to make him practice because he was always playing for real. ♪

CHAPTER 4

Elementary School Years

"Gray skies are gonna clear up, put on a happy face."

Scott sang this in his audition for his second grade class's musical production, *Wackadoo Zoo*. This song was made popular by Dick Van Dyke in *Bye Bye Birdie* many years ago. *Wackadoo Zoo* was one of the many wonderful musical opportunities Scott, at age seven, had at Mary Moore Elementary. Jacque Hall, the music teacher, had actually wanted to stage *Wackadoo Zoo* for some time but hadn't yet because of the number of songs and lines that would have to be memorized. When Scott started second grade, she thought maybe he could be the one that could bring the musical to life. Not only did Scott have the ability to memorize the extensive script, which was no small feat for a second grader, but he could also memorize and sing all the songs that came with it and sing them well. And Jacque took full advantage, assigning the other kids to different parts, with Scott in the lead role.

The performance of the musical ended up a huge success for her, the school, and us. I had parents, grandparents, and teachers telling me it was the best elementary school show they had ever seen. Some people even predicted that, one day, we would all see Scott's name in lights. ♪

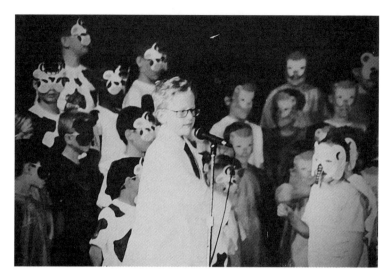

Figure 4.1 Scott playing the professor in *Wackadoo Zoo*, second-grade musical. Author's family photo.

Another opportunity arose while Scott was still seven and Lauren was thirteen: They were recruited to record with Silver Burdett & Ginn, a publishing company that produces music education books and tapes. Doug Pummell, from Silver Burdett & Ginn, approached Scott's school music teacher, Jacque Hall, after seeing an All City choir concert she directed. He asked her if she'd be willing to assemble a group of talented elementary school–aged children to record music for a school education program. Jacque recommended twelve children, including Lauren and Scott. The songs recorded were to be distributed around the country. They even got paychecks for their time.

All three of my kids participated in show choirs, musicals, orchestras, bands, and talent shows and had access to top-notch instruments and instruction before they were even out of elementary school. Scott followed in his sister's footsteps, joining show choirs, participating in talent shows and music memory competitions, and, of course, landing a lead role in *Wackadoo Zoo*.

After the success of *Wackadoo Zoo*, we started to look into more musical and acting opportunities for Scott. Soon after, we found Creative Arts Theater and School (known as CATS). Despite being located on the north side of town, which was quite a drive from our home on the south side, the school's reputation made it worth the trip, and Scott was ready to get started. After a couple of semesters of classes, where Scott honed his acting skills and gained more confidence, he decided it was time to take the next step. He was ready to audition for a show. At age nine, he auditioned for the stage play of *Annie*, about the orphan with curly red hair. He confidently took the stage like it was nothing and sang a spirited rendition of "Tomorrow." Following his performance, they had him read a few lines, told him they were done, and then asked him to leave. It seemed so abrupt, and Scott was disappointed.

He assumed that he didn't land a role. I tried to reassure him that he did a wonderful job, and that, maybe, he was too young or there would be callbacks some other time. A few days later his disappointment turned to excitement: He got several small roles in the production. From that moment on, he was hooked on musical theater.

It was at this time, the year 2000, during the show of *Annie* when Scott and Mitch Grassi met for the first time. They both played butlers among other roles, and connected over their obsession with singing. Mitch primarily did shows at Theater Arlington, another regional theater company that included adults in their productions, while Scott mainly did shows at CATS, which put on kid-only performances. But their paths would keep crossing in musically related ways around town as they both grew up. CATS soon became a regular part of Scott's incredibly busy childhood. Over several years, he added acting to his love of music. He ended up with roles in almost every show he auditioned for at CATS and eventually appeared at Theater Arlington too. Some of his credits from these companies include *The Wizard of Oz, Charlie and the Chocolate Factory, Oliver, Pocahontas, Hank and the Cowdog, Treasure Island, Haunted Theater, Hansel and Gretel,* and *It's a Wonderful Life.*

When Scott was in *Treasure Island,* the hair and makeup lady had to put a wig on him. She sarcastically said, "Why don't you just make your hair a little shorter?" The wig had to be braided into his hair, so it needed to be longer. But nine-year-old Scott took her literally and told me he needed a haircut. So we went and got him a very short haircut. It did not go well. She had to glue the wig on him every night, and apparently she told this story to kids at CATS for years.

Other than that experience, these years gave him a love of acting and the art of storytelling, and he was clearly committed to the process, no matter what he had to do to his hair. Throughout junior high and high school, Scott would talk a lot about his dream of writing musicals for Broadway. This would become real at age thirty when he collaborated with three other talented individuals, Joey Orton, Brad Silnutzer, and Petro AP. They started making skits for TikTok during the COVID-19 pandemic. He's now written three musicals, and all of them have interest from Broadway producers and television networks. It's amazing to think that this love of musicals all began at a small acting school in Arlington, Texas, sparked by a musical he performed in at Mary Moore Elementary School during second grade.

———

In addition to local theater opportunities, Scott was also interested in television opportunities. Our newspaper advertised a local audition for the children's show that Scott loved as a child, *Barney & Friends.* Scott was ecstatic about the prospect of auditioning. He received multiple callbacks for it during the audition process. The final phase involved a two-week camp, which unfortunately coincided with a prior commitment, as Scott was in another musical. I let him choose which one he wanted to do,

Figure 4.2 Musicals Scott was in at CATS. Paul Knudson

and in the end, Scott decided to honor his commitment to the musical.

One month later, in an unexpected turn of events, the *Barney & Friends* team reached back out and offered both of us an opportunity to be extras on the show. We eagerly accepted and had a blast joining the cast and crew for two episodes. It was an unforgettable experience. While taping, my thoughts went back to sweet little toddler Scott who carried around his cherished Barney dinosaur everywhere. Rather than bringing Barney with him, as he had when he was younger, Barney brought him into the wonderful world of television.

Looking back, it's easy to wonder what might have happened if he had chosen differently and attended that Barney Camp, especially once we learned that a young Selena Gomez had auditioned for the show and been cast. Still, every step of Scott's journey contributed to the artist he would become, including those brief moments on the set of *Barney & Friends* and the musical he chose instead.

———

Scott's obsessive passion for music colored his entire school experience, sometimes to the chagrin of some of his teachers. He was always an excellent student, scoring high on tests and being responsible. However his musical focus did not always have a positive effect on the classroom environment, at least according to those teachers. Scott was so wired to see music in anything that *any* topic he found interesting could trigger him, and he'd burst into song. Let's just say he was the kid who had "talks too much" on his report card when, really, the teachers meant "sings too much." As a result, he never once earned the Citizenship Award at the six-week award assemblies, which at some point almost every other kid would earn. I didn't mind entirely. I even told Scott, "You be you," which probably won't win me any parenting awards, but I really believed he couldn't help it.

I can only assume that, for some kids, his singing might even have enhanced learning. Isn't there a connection between Mozart and math? And it probably enhanced his learning. Trying to force that type of good behavior out of him might have even held him back. It's a challenge to find the balance between being unapologetically yourself and facing the constraints of societal expectations. Scott didn't have much of a filter in his younger days, but he was discovering who he was, his creativity unleashed (no tape over his mouth this time).

———

Musicals were one of many ways Scott expressed himself musically. In his younger years, he also loved country music, probably influenced by his dad. After singing at Opry's in Dallas/Fort Worth, we discovered Johnnie High's Music Review. Johnnie High was a local performer and star-maker and soon became a huge part of Scott's life. Lauren had already performed there for about two years before Scott joined her. When Scott was eight, he wanted to audition for a weekend show. That was one of the most grueling audition processes he'd done up to that point in his life. He stood in line for hours, waiting for that one small opportunity to sing for Johnnie High.

When his turn came, Scott belted out "Ace in the Hole," by George Strait. Johnnie High was so impressed that he asked Scott to perform immediately the following Saturday night.

During the first rehearsal with the band for his performance, Johnnie High abruptly stopped about four measures into the song. I wondered if something was wrong with his performance or if he had made a mistake. Scott's grandmother, who was also a vocalist, was with us at the rehearsal, and she noticed the look of concern on my face. She calmly took my hand and reassured me, "He sounds great. I really don't think anything is wrong."

Johnnie stood up and spoke to everyone at the rehearsal, explaining how surprised he was. He then said it was rare to

Figure 4.3 Scott putting on his Cowboy look. Josh Adams

hear such a young boy, especially one of Scott's age, sing that well. Johnnie recognized something in Scott and believed he had a bright future in the world of music. From then on, Scott performed fairly regularly at Johnnie High's Music Review, and Johnnie helped set in motion a series of events that would further shape Scott's musical path.

Scott and Lauren continued to find different local opportunities. It's amazing how many there were! At ages eight and fourteen, respectively, both were invited to join a group called God's Country Kids. Pamela Elliott and her daughter, Farrah, formed this children's musical ensemble with the mission of bringing joy to various communities through music. The ensemble consisted of approximately twenty young talents ages seven to eighteen, and the venues included hospitals, nursing homes, and churches. They also performed for deployed military personnel. Kacey Musgraves

Figure 4.4   Johnnie High and Scott after a Christmas show. Author's family photo.

had been a member but had recently moved to Nashville. Maren Morris was also in the group and would be a future collaborator with Pentatonix.

Pamela and Farrah saw Scott and Lauren perform at Johnnie High's Music Review. Pamela approached me at a show and said she would love to have them join the group. They would have to prepare a song or two to sing at each show, and Scott would also have the opportunity to play the piano if he wanted. Scott and

Lauren were very excited about joining the group, so I agreed to try it out and see how it went. I believed that the more they sang in front of people, the better it would be for them.

Scott and Lauren loved it and ended up singing once or twice a weekend if there were no other activities or conflicts. During the week, they would learn new songs to prepare for the shows. It taught them how to learn songs quickly, and they both ended up with a large library of songs to choose from for future shows. They would perform solos or duets, with Scott showcasing his piano skills regularly. The group became a source of smiles for many. Over the span of a decade, Pamela coordinated over one thousand shows. Scott and Lauren performed as many as they could for several years.

———

Just as Johnnie High led to God's Country Kids, it also brought us Stefani Little, another major influence on Scott and Lauren. Stefani was a regular at the Review and did both solos and background vocals for other singers in the show. She was a fantastic singer and would belt out my favorite rendition of Martina McBride's "Broken Wing." We began talking to her at the shows, and she started giving voice lessons to Scott and Lauren.

In so many ways, Stefani broadened Scott's musical world. She regularly conducted lessons in a studio owned by the actor Barry Corbin. Lauren also rehearsed there with a trio Stefani had assembled. Both kids met Corbin through this work and were even guest singers at Barry's sixtieth-birthday celebration.

Stefani also owned a company called Rhythm Nation. She regularly invited Lauren and Scott to showcase their musical talents at various local events, like Fort Worth Parade of Lights, Six Flags—Holiday in the Park, Gaylord Ice Shows, Grapefest, Grapevine's MainStreet Days, Southlake Arts in the Square, Dallas City Arts Festival, American Heart Association, City Arts

Festival @ FairPark in Dallas, Mayfest, Dallas Arboretum, and many more. Stefani always kept them informed about various local and national auditions and tried to help them succeed. Her support reached beyond the studio and lessons. She trained her students in stage presence, working with a band, audience appeal, and growing as an artist. Scott has since expressed his gratitude, and his testimonial is still on her website:

> *Thanks Stefani for teaching me how to sing, being a mentor, and providing me with countless opportunities growing up! I would not be where I am today without you. Not only are you a brilliant vocal coach, who helped me find my voice, but you also were always optimistic and I left every voice lesson feeling like I could conquer the world. Thank you!!!*

> —Scott Hoying (Pentatonix)

I have old VHS tapes of our family throughout the years, and there is one particular gem I found labeled "Family Rock" that was videotaped in 2002. This clip was probably our first foray into trying out for a reality television show. I had forgotten about it, but, watching the video more recently, I now remember how exhilarating and creative that time had been for our family. There had been a call for auditions for a show that featured musical families competing against each other. We had put together an audition tape/skit of our family, written and directed by my oldest, Lindsay. Lindsay was a Robin Leach–type British host (if anyone remembers the show *Lifestyles of the Rich and Famous*), and she introduced each member of our family and their talents. To close, Scott played piano, Rick played the guitar, and the rest of us sang our hearts out.

The show was shelved, but we did get a personal call about our audition tape. They said if the show had gone to filming, they would have picked us, but that wasn't the only reason they called. They asked if Lindsay, who wrote the script and put the video together, would be interested in moving to California and working as an intern for them in some creative department. She ultimately decided not to go, instead finishing her degree at UT Austin, but it was another proud parent moment for me and Rick. Looking back, this video is such a fun memento of our past and a fond reminder of our family bond and dynamic. ♪

⎯⎯⎯◆⎯⎯⎯

During fourth, fifth, and sixth grade, Scott's passion for music continued to expand. He joined the show choir and started playing the saxophone in the school band in sixth grade. He was pretty good on the sax and caught on quickly, probably because he could already read music and had great rhythm. But he didn't like the vibration of the mouthpiece and wasn't crazy about the bandleader. At least he didn't have to wonder whether playing the saxophone was his calling; he learned quickly that it wasn't for him.

He also maintained a strong presence in the local theater scene by participating in shows at CATS and performing in the annual talent show at school, organized by Jacque and the PE teacher, Stephanie McVey. Scott would prepare either a song to sing or a classical piano piece to play. Some of the songs included "Daycare Blues," "Yesterday," and "I'll Be There," and one year he played a beautiful rendition of "Für Elise" on the piano.

In 2001, Scott was in fourth grade and chose a LeAnn Rimes version of "God Bless America" in remembrance of the 9/11 victims of the terrorist attack on our country. It was a compelling and emotional performance. When Scott finished, he received a long-lasting standing ovation with tears streaming down many faces, mine included.

After his success with Pentatonix, Scott returned to Mary Moore one year to judge the talent show. The night of the talent show, Scott and the two other local Pentatonix members, Kirstie

Figure 4.5   Scott singing "God Bless America" at a talent show right after 9/11. Author's family photo.

and Mitch, performed a short concert, bringing Scott's journey back to where it all began. It was a full-circle moment.

Though still in fourth grade, Scott got a preview of musical life in high school when Jacque told Scott about an audition at Martin High School, which he would one day attend. It was for a production of *The Sound of Music*, and Jacque thought Scott should try out. She even spoke with the director.

There was one potential problem though. Scott was tall for his age, and height mattered in *The Sound of Music*. Each kid had to line up shorter than the previous one. When they measured him, he was barefoot, he slumped and bent his knees a little, doing anything he could to make the cut. And it all must have worked. He landed the role of Kurt in the Von Trapp family. This gave him new acting role models and a taste of theater kid culture at his future high school.

Figure 4.6 Scott playing Kurt in *The Sound of Music* at Martin High School. Paul Knudson

However, Scott didn't just take advantage of the many opportunities around him; he also created some himself. With some school friends, he created a magazine called *Cuddles: The Morphing Beaver*. Together, he and his friend developed the magazine, a newsletter of sorts, writing fun stories about Cuddles's adventures, word games, and school news.

Computer research for this project, unfortunately, taught Scott more than he wanted to know. He typed the word "cuddles the beaver" into a search engine on our home computer. . . . I was on the other side of the house when I heard a piercing scream. My ears are still ringing. I ran to the office in a panic, expecting an injury or worse. He was in the process of madly deleting the pop-up pictures. He explained what had happened, obviously shaken, and apologized. At that moment, I thought the situation was kind of funny, but I didn't think I should laugh. Instead, I used the situation as a teaching moment—one that highlighted the dangers of the internet and how best to browse online. Still, he made a similar mistake later in high school when he wanted to learn more about the movie *Dream Girls*.

Anyway, the magazine cover featured an adorable, innocent-looking superhero beaver who could change into anything. Scott and his friends sold T-shirts with a picture of Cuddles on them and held competitions. The group made hundreds of dollars in fourth grade—the beginnings of an obvious entrepreneurial spirit.

Scott became close friends with some of his magazine collaborators, whom he had actually known since kindergarten. They shared his curiosity and creative spirit and were all selected for the school's gifted and talented program. Like Scott, these close friends excelled in both music and school and would come up with the most creative ideas while playing together, pushing each other to be better.

Even though they're all in different parts of the country today, doing different things, they continue to celebrate each other's successes. What a gift to have people around you with their own dreams and goals, urging you on with support and inspiration!

As busy as Scott was, he still found time to play sports (maybe it was the name, after all). Scott's favorite sport was basketball, and he did very well in it given his height and natural athleticism. Scott had to develop some firm time-management skills to balance these commitments, though music always took precedence.

———

Scott and Lauren auditioned to sing the national anthem at the Texas Rangers baseball games when they were ten and sixteen. Scott said this was the most nervous he ever got for an audition. He felt so vulnerable since it was a cappella, and he was terrified.

It was even more terrifying when he performed it in front of a stadium of people, but it helped that Lauren was with him. They were both picked and sang as a duet and as soloists for many years, becoming fan favorites at the ballpark. Even after Lauren left for college, Scott continued as a soloist for years until he left to study music in Los Angeles.

After college, Lauren returned to the Dallas/Fort Worth area, and she continues to sing for Rangers games to this day. Some of the other places where Scott has performed the national anthem include Dallas Cowboys games, Dallas Mavericks games, NASCAR races, WWE (World Wrestling Entertainment) events, horse racing at Lone Star Park, NCAA baseball championships, and Brahma Hockey games. Meanwhile, Lauren has and still performs it at various venues herself, including professional tennis matches, circuses, and different corporate gigs. It doesn't happen as frequently now, but Lauren and Scott still sometimes reunite for a duet at a game. Chuck Morgan, the Texas Rangers' beloved public address announcer, frequently requests them for

Figure 4.7 Scott and Lauren singing the national anthem at Texas Rangers games. Author's family photo.

major games and has said on air that Lauren and Scott are his favorite national anthem singers. Mine too! ♪

———•———

Of all the local opportunities, the biggest was perhaps a competition hosted by Johnnie High, called "The Next Big Star." This was an exclusive contest, invite-only, and the prize was a trip to Nashville to record an album. There were a total of 421 contestants. It was a golden opportunity for aspiring artists, and Scott, at age twelve and in sixth grade, was among those fortunate enough to be part of it. Every Saturday for five months, twenty-one contestants would take the stage, vying for the week's top spot. This meant that over the course of twenty-one weeks, there were twenty-one winners, each standing out as the best for their respective week. The weekly champions were then called to compete against each other in a final showdown. The judges were the producers of the album: Glen Pace, Johnnie High, and two others.

There were a few kids but mostly adults competing in the finals. All twenty-one finalists performed the song they did for the week they won. Scott sang a beautiful rendition of Simon & Garfunkel's "Bridge over Troubled Water." After the performance, the judges scored the contestants, the audience voted, and Scott was announced as the winner. The prize was a dream come true. Nashville here we come!

This win resulted in *Arms around the World*, Scott's very first album, recorded, produced, mixed, and mastered by Glen Pace and Jodee Dayne at Starplex Records in Nashville. Scott received a collection of country songs written by Nashville writers, listened to each track multiple times, and after careful consideration, chose seven originals for his album. Additionally, he decided to include covers of "God Bless America," "Bridge over Troubled Water," and "Long Train Runnin'." The whole process took about a month.

Once he selected the final songs, we set up a trip to Nashville. Glen and Jodee guided us through the intricacies of the recording process. They introduced us to the band recording with Scott, and they spent days in meetings, fine-tuning every aspect of the project. When meetings were done for the day, we spent evenings visiting different parts of Nashville. Glen took us to local venues that had open mic nights, where Scott sang classics like "Unchained Melody," "Bridge over Troubled Water," and "Live Like You're Dying" (by Tim McGraw). Despite being only twelve years old, Scott was very comfortable at these venues since they were very similar to the Opry's in Texas.

The impromptu performances added some spontaneity and enjoyment to his time, a break from the intense meeting throughout the day. The atmosphere at these performance venues in Nashville was festive, and many budding artists were there to

Figure 4.8 Scott wins "The Next Big Star" contest at Johnnie High's. Josh Adams

showcase their talents. Everyone was supportive, and they treated Scott as an equal despite the age difference. Scott was loving every minute of the whole experience, immersed in making music and exploring the local country music culture.

While he was in Nashville during that first trip, the producer found out about a singing contest at the Opry Mills mall, called "Talent Search TV." Scott, with no preparation, entered the competition. The talent was incredible, likely because it was in Nashville—the center of so much music. Scott sang two of his favorite songs to perform then: "Unchained Melody" and "Bridge over Troubled Water." He ended up winning the contest. He won a guitar, which his nephew Landon now plays, and a $500 gift card.

That gift card was only for the stores in the mall, and we were leaving Nashville the next morning. With just one hour until closing time, the pressure was on to use up the card. Sure he'd have to return to Nashville soon, but why wait? We went straight to GameStop, his favorite place in the world! And he bought a PS2, Dance Dance Revolution, and a bunch of GameCube games. We raced through the aisles, laughing and buying things. To this day, it's one of his favorite childhood memories. He thought, *OMG is this what being rich is like?* It felt like we were on one of those game shows like *Supermarket Sweep* in this whirlwind of excitement and anticipation. We flew home the next day, so excited about everything that had happened.

Scott's second trip to Nashville was to lay down vocals for the album. I had to work, so only Rick accompanied him. Luckily, Rick could do his work remotely and be at all of Scott's recording sessions. Rick noted that Scott was truly in his element, fueled by his passion for music and making the songs as good as possible. He was hyperfocused. Still, he will tell you that it was an insanely intense experience. Glen would coach him on every single syllable of every word, and songs took *so* long to finish. It was good training, he insists, despite the workload. This trip ended up being about three weeks long, and they weren't able to explore Nashville so much since they had to prioritize completing the album's recordings.

As the recording sessions drew to a close, Scott returned to Texas to start seventh grade. He was so happy with the recordings, and now it was just a waiting game for the final product. Glen and Jodee brought out the best in Scott's raw talent at that age. They really went out of their way to give Scott an unforgettable experience, and we will always be grateful. Glen Pace died in September 2024. We spoke a few times while I was writing this book, and he contributed a wonderful memory for our notes section. He was such a huge part of Scott's early musical life and taught him so much about recording music. We were so sorry to hear of his passing, and I will miss our chats and catching up with each other's lives. Rest in Peace, Glen.

There was one more trip to Nashville over a long weekend for a video and photo shoot ahead of the album's release. They made sure every shot was just right and captured Scott's music and persona, resulting in long days. Watching the musical vision come to life before our eyes was exciting.

Several days after the album's completion, the producer Glen sent the songs to Johnnie High, who called me. He told me that he had just finished listening to the entire album and loved it. During our conversation, Johnnie told me Scott had the "it" factor. He said he had listened to thousands of singers over the years, and only a handful he saw had that unique quality. One such artist was LeAnn Rimes, who had done over seven hundred shows at Johnnie High's Music Review before she made it big with the song "Blue." It was challenging to explain how he identified the "it" factor, but Johnnie said that you simply recognize it when you hear it, and in Scott's case, he heard it.

The following November, exactly one year after Scott had won the contest, all the puzzle pieces fell into place. Scott had a ten-song album ready to sell and a music video too. Johnnie High celebrated the album's completion by having Scott do an hour-and-a-half show with a live band. Lauren joined him onstage for duets and did background vocals. They both did such a great job, and we were so proud of them. Many people bought albums and requested autographs. This was one of the first times he was asked for autographs, and he stayed until

Figure 4.9 Scott and Lauren singing in Scott's showcase after the CD was released. Author's family photo.

everyone who wanted one received one. Scott wanted to leave no one disappointed—a tendency he has even today, though it is much harder now.

After everything, Glen Pace offered to manage Scott. Glen had impressive credentials as a producer and extensive connections in the Nashville music scene. However, Scott was still young then, so I was hesitant to sign any long-term contracts. Rather than signing a formal contract, we devised a more informal arrangement. Glen would help secure gigs and opportunities for Scott in exchange for standard management fees of 15 percent. Scott then turned thirteen, and his voice started to change. It seemed prudent to wait because we still didn't know how this would impact him musically.

Scott's taste in music also started changing, and he was becoming more and more interested in pop music. With this in mind, there were too many uncertainties to commit to a long-term management deal.

After winning "The Next Big Star" contest in November, Johnnie invited Scott to be a part of his much-anticipated Christmas show, which was set to run for three weeks in December. For Scott, it was an incredible honor, as the show usually had some of the most accomplished talents in the area. It was going to be a lot of time and work, but what a way to kick off the holiday season. He became part of the show and started rehearsing like a seasoned musician.

Shortly after one of the Christmas shows, Johnnie once again expressed his confidence in Scott and again elaborated that he recognized something special in Scott and predicted that he would make it big in the music industry.

In 2010, the world lost a true music legend in Johnnie High. To those who had the privilege of knowing him, he was not just an entertainer but a friend and a source of support. We and so many others owe a debt of gratitude to Johnnie. Scott was on a trip with friends when he found out Johnnie died. It triggered something in him, and he said he just *bawled*. The memories of those Saturday-night shows, the excitement of "The Next Big Star" contest, the candid conversations in the greenroom with Johnnie and members of the band, the joy of being part of the Christmas shows—all those experiences and milestones in Scott's career were made possible because of Johnnie's belief in the power of music and the potential of local singers like him. Johnnie High's legacy is not just part of the history of country music but is also in those whose dreams he helped fulfill. He enjoyed helping other people shine at his iconic *Johnnie High's Country Music Revue* for more than thirty years, and the venue still showcases talents in North Texas and surrounding areas.

———

The summer after fifth grade, Scott joined his dad and some of his dad's friends on a five-week motorcycle trip to Alaska, riding as a back passenger. Honestly, I can't believe that I let Scott take that trip, but I did trust Rick who had, so far, never had an accident on the bike. Scott learned how to set up the tent right off the bat, and that became one of his daily chores. That would eventually come in handy in later years, when Scott was in college. On one occasion, he and several friends went to Coachella, a large music festival near Palm Springs. When it came time to set up the group tent, everyone except Scott was at a loss. He set it up like a pro, to the amazement of all his friends. All those nights on the road to Alaska paid off.

One of Rick's friends on the trip, Howard, was trying to learn how to play the harmonica. He unsuccessfully attempted to learn some simple songs, so Scott asked him if he could try. I don't think Howard expected too much from an eleven-year-old. Scott messed around for a bit on the instrument and then started to play some songs. Rick joined in, and they started jamming together. Howard never picked up the harmonica again, instead giving it to Scott. Jamming became a nightly event around the campfire.

"Born to Be Wild" was a favorite, which Pentatonix would later perform on Hard Rock Night during *The Sing-Off*.

During this trip to Alaska, I got a phone call, and the person on the other end identified himself as the Canadian border patrol. At first, I thought Rick put one of his friends up to make the call. However, he began to ask several questions about Scott and whether or not I gave my husband permission to take Scott out of the United States. He wanted to make sure Scott wasn't kidnapped. Glad I didn't continue to think of it as a prank and say the wrong thing. The trip might have ended with Rick in jail. Yikes!

After five weeks and a 3,500-mile ride, Scott and Rick stopped in Seattle. The plan was to ship the motorcycle back and then fly home. As they were getting ready to turn left, safe and sound at the shipment facility, they suddenly heard very loud screeching tires. A truck was coming up behind them.

Figure 4.10 Scott and his dad riding a motorcycle in Alaska. Author's family photo.

Thank God the truck managed to stop a few feet behind them, and they were fine. Another disaster averted. Despite my justified concerns, Scott later told me that the trip "was probably the most intense, life-changing, formative five weeks of my childhood and could probably be an entire chapter. *So* many stories. The bears, parks, I journaled every night. I slept on a pool float and would listen to bears pass my tent, praying I didn't get eaten. We almost hit a big-ass moose once. I would fall asleep holding Dad as we drove through mountains. One time, one of the other motorcyclists made fun of me, so I ran away for like an *hour* so they'd think I was missing. Also, they tried to extend the trip, and I had a *meltdown*. Great trip, but I was ready to go home."

So they did.

But he wouldn't be home for long! Shortly after "The Next Big Star" contest, auditions came to Dallas for a TV reality show called *Star Search*. This was a show that ran from 1983 to 1995 and had dozens of stars on it before they became famous; it was rebooted in 2003. Scott auditioned in Dallas, singing "Bridge over Troubled Water."

About a week later, we got the call. The casting director, Sharon Nash, let us know that Scott had made the cut. He would be on national television. And in a few months, he'd be heading to Hollywood.

Going to Hollywood for the show was surreal. We felt like VIPs. They flew us out and settled us in a hotel near the iconic Walk of Fame. As we explored our new surroundings, we couldn't help but notice Arsenio Hall's star on the Walk of Fame. He was set to be the host of the new *Star Search*. Just two decades later, Scott would have his own star with Pentatonix on that very street, not even a half mile away.

Figure 4.11 We found Arsenio Hall's star on the Hollywood Walk of fame a day before we met him on the set of *Star Search*. Twenty years later, Scott would have a star with Pentatonix just a mile away. Author's family photo.

Scott, now preparing for the show, was in for a roller coaster of rehearsals, interviews, and preparations. He wanted to sing the Simon & Garfunkel tune for the televised show, but they said that was not possible because they couldn't get approval for the song. I suggested "I'll Be There," a Jackson 5 song he occasionally sang at events. Lindsay pointed out that Michael Jackson had been in the news recently, for some ugly accusations, so it might be inappropriate. Finally, Scott settled on a Billy Gilman song called "There's a Hero." ♪

Figure 4.12 Scott and Arsenio Hall at *Star Search*. Author's family photo.

Scott was up in the first round against a lovely girl named Karina Pasian. She ended up singing a cover of "I'll Be There," the song Scott almost picked. The Billy Gilman song was much less known and may have played a role in Scott's loss. While he did get some nice feedback from one of the judges, Naomi Judd, who commented on his talent and perfect pitch, he lost out to Karina in that very first round, ending up in dead last place. Lindsay felt so bad that she had advised him not to pick the Jackson song. But there was so much talent, and competition was fierce. Several of the kids on that season have established themselves successfully in the industry. Karina is still singing successfully, and the winner

Figure 4.13 When Pentatonix received their star on the Walk of Fame. Author's family photo.

that season actually ended up being David Archuleta, a future *American Idol* runner-up. Clearly, it wasn't Lindsay's fault.

Scott recovered quickly, and if anything, the experience made him even more excited about the possibilities in the industry. His positive attitude is one of the big reasons he is successful. Even if things didn't go as planned and no matter how often he was told no by a casting agent or someone else, his dedication *never* changed. He always appreciated the experiences for what they were, learned from them, and kept moving forward. It's inspired me as his mom, and I try to be more like him in my life, even now.

So many stars have faced similar defeats on *Star Search* or elsewhere before finding their success. Setbacks can always be used to learn and find new ways to move forward. And Scott was in good company—Beyoncé, Justin Timberlake, and Dave Chappelle were on the first episode of the original *Star Search* show and did not win, along with LeAnn Rimes, Christina Aguilera, Usher, and Britney Spears, just to name a few. In the end, it didn't feel like a loss to Scott. He was on TV, and he was more devoted. His teachers back at his old elementary school would agree. To commemorate the *Star Search* occasion, they got together, purchased a star, and named it after him. A real star!!

Two decades later, in 2021, the *Star Search* winner David Archuleta and Scott created an amazing TikTok together, singing "Hallelujah." They also both appeared on *The Masked Singer* in the same season in 2023: David got second place, and Pentatonix got third. It's interesting how their musical paths continue to cross. David even opened for Pentatonix during their summer tour in 2024.

———

Scott had a lot of trusted teachers and supporters who helped him grow as a musician. One teacher helped him by letting him go. At the end of the sixth grade, Keli Ferrier, who had taught him piano for seven years, recognized it was time for their lessons to end. He had progressed beyond her. She confided in me that she now had to practice before Scott's lessons. She also no longer had the time to do that, since she had started a full-time job as the head choir instructor at a new high school. Keli suggested we find a college professor or a professional musician with the expertise needed to help Scott reach his potential. Despite Scott's affection for Keli, it was time to move on. We just needed to find the right fit.

Scott's vocal instructor introduced us to a seasoned jazz pianist, Julie Bonk. After one lesson, we immediately knew we had found the perfect teacher. Scott took lessons from Julie starting at age twelve and stayed with her throughout high school. I can't help but wonder if Grandma Bottens was watching over us and nudged us in the direction of jazz, knowing it would take Scott

Figure 4.14 Scott and Julie Bonk at a gig. Author's family photo.

to the next level. Perhaps it was my own memories of her playing jazz tunes on the piano that led me to realize Julie was the right choice. Julie helped Scott unlock new horizons of learning and creativity. She helped solidify Scott's technical abilities and taught him improvisation and the many nuances of jazz. His abilities grew beyond just the black and white keys of the piano, and he developed a strong understanding of music theory.

Julie would frequently invite Scott to perform as a guest artist at her gigs. With each performance, he learned a little more about the importance of stage presence and entertaining his audience. She believed that teaching was so much more than just practicing and, through her, Scott became a well-rounded musician.

Julie and Scott also composed together, writing a beautiful song called "Coming Home." It was a very emotional song about a silhouette of a man at the door and a wife who doesn't know if the figure is a soldier with sad news or her husband coming home. In the end, it's her husband at the door. The song spotlights the sacrifices our military makes to protect our freedom.

Through Julie, Scott also got to know Norah Jones, a Grammy-winning singer and pianist, probably best known for her song "Don't Know Why." She was Julie's student as well. Over the years, Scott and Norah have occasionally appeared on various television shows at the same time. Whenever that happens, I like to reach out to Julie. She has such an evident joy and pride in them and their impact on the musical world.

CHAPTER 5

Junior High Years

Laura Farnell, Scott's choir teacher at Boles Junior High, can still recall her initial meeting with Scott when he tried out for show choir as an incoming seventh grader: "I vividly remember the first time I met Scott as a sixth grader. I'd already heard about him from his elementary school teacher [Jacque Hall] and was really excited to have him a part of the choir and show choir. He came into the room, announced his song, and I remember asking if he had an accompaniment track or if he'd be singing a cappella, and he said, 'I'll be playing my own accompaniment.' He stepped to the piano and started the piece, and I knew at that moment that I was in for quite a ride getting to teach such a special student, musician, performer, and young man. I couldn't quit smiling!"

———

In junior high, Scott was in basketball and track, was a member of the Junior National Honor Society, and maintained excellent grades. He balanced all that with his time in choir and other musical activities, including the University Interscholastic League (UIL) sight-reading contest, all-region auditions, solo and ensemble contests, and talent shows.

I remember when Scott auditioned for the all-region choir in seventh grade. I waited anxiously outside the audition room while he went to perform the required pieces. When he came out, I asked how it went. He said it went well, but the judge had told him something that still sticks with Scott all these years later. She said there was no doubt that music would always be a part of Scott's life and asked him to promise that he would always sing for good.

In 2004, when Scott was about thirteen, Pamela, who was the director of God's Country Kids, asked him to join Radio Disney Superstars, which eventually transitioned into Radio Disney Superstar Express. It was a group of very talented junior high–aged kids who, at some point, had won or were runners-up in various vocal competitions. His sister Lauren was eighteen and had just left for college, so it was Scott's first time joining a group outside of school without her. Radio Disney Superstars was a bit different from God's Country Kids, and it also had more reach and impact. The shows were choreographed and very professional. They practiced several times a week, but even with Scott's busy schedule and homework, he always made sure he could make it to practice. They recorded music and even sold CDs; their performances were also more diverse and at bigger venues.

Scott and the group traveled nationwide, performing at Disney World, corporate events, and schools across Texas. They even opened for the Doobie Brothers at a fair in Texas and the Jonas Brothers at Hawaiian Falls. Scott was paid for each show he did, prompting us to open a bank account in his name. Over time, he saved a substantial sum of money, which became his primary source of spending money his freshman year of college. I am so grateful for Pamela Elliott; she was driven and utterly devoted to these kids and their talent, and she showed them glimpses of what was possible in music in the future.

Figure 5.1 Scott performing at a Radio Disney show. Author's family photo.

At one of Pamela Elliot's Christmas shows, Scott was performing Mariah Carey's classic, "All I Want for Christmas Is You." Scott's voice was in the middle of that awkward change that comes with adolescence, and on one of the high notes, he cracked. As the show ended and the crowd began to leave, a man approached me. He introduced himself as Tom McKinney. He talked about Scott's voice and the performance. He seemed to possess a wealth of knowledge about vocal technique and believed he could help Scott through the challenges of his changing voice. Tom said he was certified in a specific technique for singers going through puberty and the changing voice. ♪

Tom called this technique "Singing with Ease of Speech" which is a method that promises not only to enhance vocal abilities but also to protect the voice during extended performances, such as a concert. Tom believed that by mastering this technique, Scott would be able to tackle the demanding high notes and build his vocal endurance for longer performances. It was a skill set that, according to Tom, would be invaluable as Scott pursued a professional singing career.

In fact, Tom introduced Beyoncé and Solange Knowles to this particular singing style, and at one point, he even connected their father/manager, Matthew Knowles, with Scott.

Scott and I were both curious to see what Tom could do, so Scott began taking lessons from him almost immediately. In just weeks, we could already tell there was a difference in his voice. Before long, Scott's voice gained new clarity and strength, and the cracks had completely disappeared. His range became so much larger, particularly in his chest and head voices, and he was hitting high notes with ease.

As Scott got older, he started singing more often and for longer amounts of time, particularly when Pentatonix started. Scott's ability to sing for hours to this day is entirely credited to Tom and the "Singing with Ease of Speech" technique. It's amazing how a moment of vulnerability or a chance meeting can become a stepping stone for growth.

A quote on Tom's website from Scott:

I would not have the voice I have today without Tom.

—Scott Hoying (Pentatonix)

———

The spring talent show in seventh grade was an exciting moment for Scott, who was still focused on country music at the time. He had just completed the album from the Johnnie High contest. Scott's choir teacher, Laura, aware of Scott's country album, approached him with a proposition. She asked him if he would be interested in performing some of his songs at the talent show, offering the added bonus of selling his CDs at the event. Scott was excited about the idea of once again sharing his own music with a live audience.

The night of the talent show arrived, and Scott took the stage with a mix of nervousness and anticipation. He sang a few of his favorite songs from the album while also playing the piano. He knocked it out of the park, and afterward, CDs began flying off our makeshift merch table. Unexpectedly, that event turned into a sudden whirlwind of autograph and picture requests. It was a wild night for a seventh grader. He connected with an appreciative audience even though his music was unfamiliar to most of them and even made a little pocket money from his CD sales on the side.

———

Scott's eighth-grade activities were pretty much the same as the prior year—except for one major change: Mitch Grassi. Mitch, who would become a founding member of Pentatonix, was now at the same junior high. Although Mitch was a year behind Scott, they were in the same choirs. They already knew each other from being in *Annie* together, but it had been a while since they had seen each other. Their friendship picked up where it had left off at CATS, and they became good friends again. Laura told me she was one lucky choir director to have two great singers: a baritone and tenor, both of superstar quality.

Scott and Mitch were obviously obsessed with music, and they had a lot of fun in choir together. Scott told me that he and Mitch used to rewrite choir songs with funny lyrics, cracking themselves up in the process. They also bonded on a bus trip with the choir, sitting together, each with an iPod, listening and singing along to several Daft Punk songs. Scott's memory of singing those songs with Mitch on the bus sparked an idea years later, when Pentatonix was considering recording a Daft Punk song: and Scott said, "Why not do several?" In 2015, their mashup of Daft Punk songs ended up winning Pentatonix its first Grammy.

High School Years

Eventually, music won out over sports. In high school, Scott played basketball his freshman year but soon realized he did not have the bandwidth to do everything he wanted. The following year he decided to step away from basketball and fully commit himself to his music, including preparation for All State, which was the yearly assembly of talented choral singers throughout Texas, which had become his primary obsession by this stage. He made this prestigious All State choir his sophomore, junior, and senior years, missing out on his freshman year—getting cut in the last round.

He was heavily involved in several choirs, including his class choir, show choir, and chamber choir. All were led by Kay Owens, a fantastic choir teacher the kids all loved. Like Laura, the junior high teacher, Kay let the kids hang out in her class-room during lunch and after school. It was the focus of his social world—friends singing together and having fun with and around music. Scott also won the "Martin High School Idol" contest his freshman year.

During those years, he continued developing his piano skills. Heavily influenced by Julie, Scott became the Martin High School Jazz Band pianist, garnering many accolades and awards. Scott received "Outstanding Jazz Musician" and "Outstanding

Figure 6.1 Kay Owens and the Texas All-Staters. Author's family photo.

Musicianship" awards several times throughout his sophomore, junior, and senior years. In 2009, the Jazz band, MHS Band, Choir, and Orchestra collectively won a High School Signature Grammy Award, and the prize was $10,000. I guess this might count as his first Grammy—before Pentatonix!

Scott remained a dedicated student. He was in Advanced Placement (AP) courses and consistently excelled in them. He met Kirstie Maldonado, the second of his future Pentatonix collaborators, on the first day of school in AP English. He instantly became obsessed with her. He said she was sweet, bubbly, and very funny, and they quickly formed a strong friendship and even dated for about six months, remaining inseparable throughout much of high school. Kirstie actually dated Mitch, too, for a short time. These three friends truly have a deep-seated bond that can't be broken.

Scott's leadership abilities started to shine in high school. He was elected Junior Class President, and his teachers nominated him for HOBY, which stood for Hugh O'Brian Youth

Figure 6.2 Kirstie and Scott in high school. Author's family photo.

Leadership, an organization dedicated to inspiring and developing a global community of youth and volunteers focused on leadership, service, and innovation. He also served his local community by going to Mission Arlington, which helped out families in need. His favorite part of that work was interpreting for Hispanic people who didn't know English. He took Spanish all through high school and enjoyed practicing his skills and teaching them English.

———

Scott's time at CATS marked the beginning of a friendship with Caroline Kraddick, the daughter of the legendary radio figure Kidd Kraddick. Scott was thirteen and Caroline was fifteen when they first became close friends as actors in the musical *The Wizard of Oz*. Scott had a bit of a crush on Caroline. They would hang out together at rehearsals every free minute. Even though this was the only musical Caroline did with Scott at CATS, their friendship was solid and would continue with or without Dorothy and the Cowardly Lion.

Caroline and Scott went to different high schools, but Scott would head over to Caroline's house after school, and they'd spend hours around the piano, belting out tunes as if they were auditioning for a reality show. They even entered a vocal competition together, singing a beautiful duet called "The I Love You Song" for the "Teen Talent Follies." When Scott decided he wanted to take their friendship up a notch, he asked Kidd for permission to take Caroline to a movie. Kidd paused for a minute but responded yes, as long as he could accompany them. Then Kidd had an even better idea: "How about I take you and Caroline to an Imogen Heap concert?"

Scott, a huge Imogen Heap fan, jumped at the chance. Kidd got them backstage after the show to meet her, and Scott couldn't stop talking about it for weeks. At the time, Imogen Heap was changing pop and electropop music, and she was such an inspiration for Scott. Much later, they would become friends through Randy Jackson after meeting about a potential project Randy

Figure 6.3   Scott and Caroline Kraddick in *The Wizard of Oz*. Paul Knudson

was organizing. Funny story: In summer 2024, Imogen invited Scott to a banquet, telling him it was mermaid themed. He misunderstood this to mean that he should dress mermaid-like and showed up in a see-through mesh shirt to a black-tie event that had mermaid-themed decorations. He was initially embarrassed but there was not much he could do, and he didn't want to leave, so he just went with it.

Scott and Caroline had other adventures together, one of which was later musical inspiration. Riding in Caroline's car, they got a flat tire and were stranded on the side of the road. Caroline asked Scott if he knew how to change a tire, and he responded, "I've never done it, but I will try." What followed was a hilarious scene of Scott fumbling with the jack and lug wrench and Caroline offering "helpful tips" from the sidelines. Eventually, Scott called his dad and asked him to come to the rescue. Fortunately, they were close to our house. Seizing the opportunity, Rick turned the situation into a teaching moment. He showed Scott and Caroline step-by-step how to change the tire, so they would both know what to do in the future. It was one of many instances that probably inspired Scott's song, "Call My Dad," about always being able to call his dad when he needed help. It was released on Father's Day in June 2024.

Even after they both graduated from high school, Scott stayed in touch with Caroline, and Scott still occasionally does interviews on *The Kidd Kraddick Morning Show*. Not only does that demonstrate an ongoing connection to Caroline, but the show was also one of Scott's earliest outlets as a composer!

When he was a freshman in high school, getting ready for school and listening to Kidd Kraddick's radio show, Scott heard something that made his heart race. Kidd announced a contest to create a new jingle for a fundraiser supporting his charity, Kidd's Kids, which organized all-expense-paid trips to Walt Disney World for children with life-threatening conditions and their families. Contestants had to submit a recording of themselves singing to the radio station, and Kidd would select the top six entries.

Scott bolted down the stairs and excitedly told me about it. Without hesitation, he decided to participate. As soon as he returned home from school later that day, Scott wasted no time and recorded a soulful rendition of "Georgia on my Mind," accompanying himself on the piano. He poured his heart and soul into it and rushed to the post office to mail his entry. A week later, the thrilling news arrived: Scott was one of the six finalists selected by Kidd himself! Kidd's radio audience would choose the ultimate winner, but there was still much more to do.

The group of six gathered on a Saturday, and the day kicked off with Kidd's announcement: "Like with any good contest, there is a twist." The twist? Each of them had ten minutes to write a jingle and perform it a cappella. Only five would advance, while one was sent home. One of the contestants had brought a songwriter with her, but she had to go to the room alone and write it herself. She was the one who was sent home. Scott made it through, and they broke for lunch.

The tension ratcheted up after lunch. Kidd placed them in individual rooms, each with a CD containing three music tracks. They had one hour to create a full jingle without any help. They had cameras on them the entire time, so Scott tried to look calm and relaxed. But his insides were churning. After the hour was up, they had to go into the studio and record their jingle. Kidd, Kellie, Big Al, Psycho Shannon, and the other radio show cohosts picked the top three.

Scott made it to the next round. A week later, Scott and the two other finalists visited the Irving, Texas, radio station. The show was from 6 a.m. to 9 a.m., so we had to arrive very early. Kidd introduced them on air, and they each performed their jingle live. Kidd encouraged the listening audience to call in with their votes. At first, votes were evenly divided between the three, but soon, Scott began to pull ahead as votes for the other contestants started to slow down. Despite his growing lead, my nerves were on edge. The hour of voting seemed like an eternity.

Scott emerged as the winner, and his jingle became an annual tradition for years, playing every fall during the Kidd's Kids Trip charity fundraising drive.

Another jingle contest prize was the honor of recording an original song in a professional studio. Kidd would feature the song on his show. Kidd enlisted the services of a professional songwriter and producer, Robi Menace, and an engineer/producer known as Big Phazz. Kidd also rented out the Maximedia recording studio in Dallas. Hal Fitzgerald, who owned the studio, mixed and mastered the song.

Once Scott learned the original song, we all met at Maximedia Studio so he could start recording. Robi, the producer, threw

Scott a curveball: he suggested Scott lie on the studio floor to record. It was a strange idea, and Scott hesitated but decided to trust Robi and try it.

At first, it seemed like a novel idea, but as the session continued, Scott realized he needed to stand for those powerful high notes and finished the session standing up. Scott didn't understand it at the time, but looking back on it, he thinks Robi just wanted him to relax.

Scott had to go to the studio twice to get the song perfect. During the second studio session, we had an unexpected surprise. When we arrived, we crossed paths with the singer Mary J. Blige on her way out. Scott wanted to talk to her, but she was surrounded by her entourage and appeared to be in a rush, so he decided against it. It was still encouraging, working in the same space as a major star!

———

After a collaborative recording session with the talented sound engineer Big Phazz, Scott found himself presented with another opportunity. Big Phazz, also known for his songwriting and producing skills, invited Scott to record two of his original compositions, "Hey Kim" and "If I Could My Way," at his studio, Top of the Line. Scott also caught the attention of songwriter JoJo Davis, who had heard him perform on Kidd's show. Impressed by his talent, JoJo reached out with a proposal: They would write a song together, and if it turned out well, JoJo would cover the recording costs. They ended up creating a fantastic song, "Memories," and soon found themselves in the recording studio, bringing it to life. It ended up on two of Scott's future albums. What began as a simple jingle recording for Kidd's fundraiser had evolved into recording five songs. Many of these tracks would eventually find their way onto Scott's early albums, especially his self-titled album *Scott Hoying*, marking the beginning of a significant part of his music career.

Weeks later, Kidd reached out to Scott and asked him if he would be interested in doing a musical project together. Kidd wanted to gauge Scott's interest in arranging and recording a song he had written, titled "This Is Your Moment." It is a beautiful song about what can happen when you take the initiative to put yourself out there. Kidd felt that Scott would be a good fit for it. He certainly had lived it, over and over again, putting himself out there in various competitions and spotlight performances.

Scott arranged the composition and recorded the vocals but felt something was missing. He recommended adding a choir to fill it out vocally. So Kidd enlisted the St. Paul's Praise Team to add some dimension and depth to the song. This full choral sound would later become almost a trademark in Scott's work. "This Is Your Moment" turned out truly special and ended up on two of Scott's CDs.

———

Fun Fact: Scott participated in a documentary series titled *Choral Singing in America: Nurturing this Country's Soul*. It premiered virtually and in person at Wheaton College, Illinois, on February 3, 2024.

After "This Is Your Moment" was completed, Kidd expressed an interest in managing Scott's career. He recognized Scott's talent and potential in the music industry. The management deal ultimately didn't work out, but the two remained close, and Kidd, having considerable experience in the music industry, took on the role of a mentor. He provided Scott with invaluable advice, guiding him as he navigated the complexities of the industry. One key area of Kidd's counsel was the types of people to avoid. The music industry, known for its competitive and sometimes cutthroat nature, can be challenging for newcomers. Kidd knew that. He helped Scott steer clear of individuals and situations that could be detrimental to his career.

Through their friendship, Scott gained insights and knowledge beyond the typical artist-manager relationship. Kidd's mentorship was instrumental in helping Scott build a solid foundation in the music business, giving him the tools and awareness needed to make informed decisions.

Scott would frequently be on Kidd's show and was often invited to various events hosted by Kidd. One notable event was Kidd's annual Christmas party, attended by his family, friends, cohosts, and station employees. Kidd asked Scott to perform at the party one year, playing the piano and singing holiday tunes. Rick and I were thrilled when Kidd included us on the invite list. During the party, Scott entertained everyone with his piano playing and soulful singing. After his heartfelt rendition of "Silent Night," Big Al, one of the cohosts of *Kidd's Morning Show*, stood up and loudly praised Scott. The room erupted in applause and laughter, clearly in agreement.

Another memorable moment from the evening was a beautiful duet between Scott and Caroline, an original song Scott wrote called "Waiting." The party was filled with music, joy, and heartfelt performances, making it an unforgettable night.

—————

The ripple effect of the jingle contest extended even further. I received a phone call from a booking agent in the Stephen Sondheim Theater for the Performing Arts at the Fairfield Arts and Convention Center, in Iowa. Having heard of Scott through Kidd's show, the agent invited Scott to their venue to perform. We drove from our home in Texas to Fairfield, Iowa. At just fifteen years old, Scott put on an hour-long show with only him and a piano. It was the longest he'd ever performed without a break, but he did a wonderful job. Rick and I were so impressed by his poise and self-assurance at that young age. What made the experience even more meaningful was that Fairfield was only an hour from my hometown of Fort Madison, Iowa. Scott was on spring break, so we had a chance to see and reconnect with family and friends. The next morning, the local newspaper published an article about him performing in Fairfield. It was especially meaningful for a local like me!

———

Kidd Kraddick had several contests over the years, and Scott enthusiastically entered most of them. In Scott's senior year, Kidd had a contest in which the prize was meeting the cast of *Glee*, a top-rated TV musical series that Scott loved. Scott got together with his friends Kirstie and Mitch to work on a song for the contest. They arranged an a cappella version of Lady Gaga's hit, "Telephone," and submitted it to the competition. Sadly, they didn't end up winning the contest, but their version did not go unnoticed.

Their choir teacher, Kay Owens, heard about the performance and invited them to perform it in the year-end choir concert of Scott and Kirstie's senior year (Mitch was a junior). Someone recorded their version and uploaded it to YouTube, and it quickly

Figure 6.4 Scott, Kirstie, and Mitch as The Trio, in high school. Author's family photo.

went viral. This was Scott's first experience with a viral YouTube video, and it was pretty exciting. This was the earliest manifestation of what would become Pentatonix, though, at the time, they called themselves The Trio. ♪

Once again, Scott's journey was proving that sometimes, connections and opportunities arise when you take a leap of faith and pursue your passions wholeheartedly, even if you don't literally win something. Never underestimate the importance of making meaningful connections and following your artistic instincts.

Sadly, Kidd Kraddick died of a cardiovascular event while attending one of his Kidd Kid's fundraisers. Kidd's legacy lives on through the Kidd Kraddick Foundation, which his daughter, Caroline, oversees. His cohosts still host his show, now called the *Kidd Kraddick Morning Show*, and they continue to support and showcase new talent.

Thank you, Kidd, for everything you did for Scott. We will always remember the talks, phone calls, emails, meetings, advice, and so much more. Your guidance and support were invaluable, and I will always feel your impact. We miss you, Kidd, and I still think about the quote you would say every day at the end of your show: "Keep looking up, 'cause that's where it all is."

———

In Mansfield, Texas, Scott won another opportunity to record an EP with four songs. He didn't care about the winning part—he just wanted to sing. In the finals, Scott sang against another young, talented singer who had never recorded, and Scott really wanted her to win. He'd already recorded previously and was happy with his performance. He was willing just to walk away. It was lovely of him, but I did not think that withdrawing or doing worse on purpose would have been the right thing to do. He stayed in the contest and won. He recorded four songs from that contest, including "Georgia on My Mind," "Take It Back," and "Good-Bye."

Figure 6.5 Scott and Kidd Kraddick at a Christmas party. Author's family photo.

There was also the "Jennifer Hudson Contest." A radio show held this contest in downtown Dallas, and the prize was a chance to sing with Jennifer Hudson. A sixteen-year-old Scott heard about the opportunity over the radio and went for it. He loved Jennifer Hudson and could quote her breakout movie *Dreamgirls* from start to finish (he had done his research, remember). We made our way to the contest venue, where at least one hundred other competitors had gathered, with three judges presiding. Scott waited excitedly to sing, and finally, when his name was called, he stepped forward. He belted out a soulful rendition of "And I Am Telling You I'm Not Going," which was a good choice considering Jennifer Hudson sang that in *Dreamgirls*.

The three judges and fellow contestants gave him a standing ovation. It was such a supportive community, and the camaraderie was genuinely heartwarming. Scott was one of the finalists, but now it was time for people to vote online. The voting lasted for a week. Then he received a call from the radio station announcing that he had won! He was ecstatic and couldn't wait to meet

Jennifer and sing with her. Unfortunately, he received some sad news just two days before he was supposed to meet with her; the concert was canceled because of the spread of swine flu. Scott was heartbroken.

He did get to meet her several years later when they collaborated on "How Great Thou Art," on one of Pentatonix's Christmas albums. He also sang with her in October 2023 while on her talk show.

———

When Scott turned sixteen, he was finally old enough to follow in Jennifer Hudson's footsteps and audition for *American Idol*. It had been his dream to audition since the show started when he was eleven, and he was beyond excited. However, reality TV shows presented a different set of challenges.

The auditions didn't come to Texas that year, so we drove to the Kansas City auditions. He made it through the first round. About a month later, we headed back to Kansas City, and he made it through the second round; then the same day, he went to the final audition before going to the live show in front of the judges at the time: Simon Cowell, Randy Jackson, and Paula Abdul.

This final round included the executive producer, who commented that while Scott was talented, he just didn't have an interesting enough backstory. This was probably the most upset I'd seen Scott. He'd been waiting for this opportunity for so long just to be told that he was good but not interesting. This scenario repeated itself the next few years, with the same producer giving the final rejection. The last time Scott auditioned, the producer remembered him and told him that he was not right for the show, the subtext being that he should not return.

Scott understood that he would never make the show with that producer in charge, so he decided to look elsewhere, at least until there was a new producer. As luck would have it, a couple of years later *The Sing-Off* happened, and he no longer needed *American Idol.*

———

In 2006, Caleb Cameron and RJ Knapp, who had recently graduated from Belmont University in Nashville, contacted us and wanted to meet regarding Scott and recording his music. They told me that JoJo Davis suggested they consider recording Scott. They had already listened to the song Scott cowrote and recorded with JoJo, "Memories," and were enthusiastic about the idea of working with him.

Their enthusiasm was contagious. Caleb and RJ were very knowledgeable about recording music, so we agreed. Scott, at age fifteen, and Rick traveled to Nashville to meet up with them and record. They decided on a five-song EP with originals from both parties, including rerecording "Memories." Scott enjoyed the process and was encouraged to contribute his own thoughts and ideas. It was a melting pot of musical innovation and collaboration, and we were thrilled with the end result. They titled the EP *Currently Single*, and it was a fun mix of Scott, Caleb, and RJ's creative visions which introduced Scott to new ideas and musical concepts.

During that trip, Caleb introduced Scott to an up-and-coming artist, Jazmine Sullivan, just as she released her album, *Fearless*. Scott's musical taste changed overnight. He hadn't been exposed to R&B, and he thought her voice and musicality were so cool and different—there was so much emotion behind her sound. He immediately became obsessed with her and searched for other singers with unique and soulful voices such as Beyoncé and John Legend. His singing also changed, not just what he sang but how he sang. To this day, Scott credits Caleb for changing the direction of his musical tastes.

Caleb and RJ ended up offering to manage Scott. They had skills as songwriters, recording engineers, and producers, and Scott enjoyed his time with them so much that we decided to sign a contract. However, fate intervened, and shortly after the release of *Currently Single*, they had an opportunity in Houston and relocated. Due to the distance and other competing obligations, everyone agreed that their work together should be put on hold.

———

There were other notable music managers interested in working with Scott. Among them was Matthew Knowles, probably better known as Beyoncé's dad. In 2007, Scott's voice teacher, Tom McKinney, operated one of his voice studios at Matthew's studio, where he taught vocal lessons to various students, including Beyoncé and her sister, Solange. Tom urged Matthew to listen to Scott's vocal abilities and gave him some of Scott's recordings. This eventually led to an invitation from Matthew Knowles to fly Scott, Rick, and me to Houston for a day at his studio.

Scott had recently gotten into pop/R&B thanks to Caleb Cameron, and Beyoncé quickly became one of his favorite artists. To his disappointment, Beyoncé was not there, but the day was still so energizing for him. Scott got to see Beyoncé's awards and even got to hold one of her Grammys.

While we were there, we met Bianca Ryan and her manager, Sharon Nash. Bianca won the first *America's Got Talent* competition at the age of eleven. Interestingly, Sharon was also the casting director the year Scott was on *Star Search*. The entertainment world was getting smaller. Both Scott and Bianca showcased their talents, singing several songs under Matthew Knowles's guidance.

Right after Scott and Bianca sang several songs at Matthew's studio, he said he wanted to sign both of them. Scott was thrilled, until Matthew elaborated that he wanted both of them to go in the direction of Christian music. He was sure he could get him signed with a Christian label. At this time, Scott was more inclined to go the direction of pop or R&B music, so he declined the offer. Scott sings a lot of Christmas music to this day, so Matthew was not too far off.

In 2008, we met David Lambert at an event called "Exposure Showcase," which was specifically for industry professionals to scout and/or network. Scott sang and did some acting at the event. Afterward, David, an award-winning voice-over artist, professional actor, and audio engineer, reached out to Scott and invited him to come record in his studio for free, and Scott accepted. David was an expert audio engineer and could teach and introduce Scott to some of the more technical aspects of recording with an impressive attention to detail. For fun, they recorded "Let It Be," "That's What I Like about You," and several others. After working with David for a while, Scott decided to do a self-titled album, combining some new recordings with previous ones. Scott asked David to record some specific songs. David agreed and recorded "Georgia on My Mind" and "Wrong Ticket," an original song written with a high school friend, Kellie Nicholas.

He went to Big Phazz and asked to record an original "Good-Bye." This was one of my favorites. In it, Scott paired lyrics with "Für Elise," the Beethoven classic he played when he was younger.

He added previously recorded songs, "Hey Kim" and "This Is Your Moment," recorded and produced by Big Phazz and Robi Menace, and songs from the album *Currently Single*, which included three more of his originals: "Waiting," "Distant Face," and "Memories." The album had a diverse selection of songs, showcasing multiple musical influences and collaborations.

———

Scott was still without management, but that was about to change. In 2009, Marty Rendleman called us up, and I immediately knew who she was. She was known for clients like LeAnn Rimes, Mikaila, and *American Idol* finalist Kristy Lee Cook. Marty told me that Kidd Kraddick had called her and recommended she consider managing Scott. She wanted to meet Scott for a chat and to listen to some of his music. If it was a good fit, she wanted to discuss potential management opportunities.

Excited by her interest in Scott, we quickly agreed to meet with her a few days later. During the meeting, she discussed her experience and Scott's potential, and what she could do for him. Marty was also naturally witty, and she made us laugh. Scott played and sang several songs for her, and by the end of the meeting, Marty made us an offer. We were so impressed by Marty's demeanor and what she brought to the table that we decided to sign with her shortly after that meeting.

Almost immediately, Scott was back in the recording studio. Scott recorded several songs, mostly originals, under Rendleman Management. This album's main recording engineers and producers were Josh Goode and Bradley Prakope.

Josh and Bradley produced seven of the songs for the album: "Take it Back," "Waiting for You" and "Good-Bye," which were rerecorded originals written by Scott; "He's Just Not into You" and "Don't Go Now," written by all three; and covers of "Georgia on My Mind" and "Bridge over Troubled Water." Marty also got Scott a publishing deal with BMI Publishing to protect Scott's songs.

During a trip out to LA, Marty introduced Scott to Seth Riggs, known as the vocal coach to the stars (some clients over the years included Michael Jackson, Stevie Wonder, and Ray Charles). Seth asked Scott to play and sing a song on the piano, and Scott chose "Georgia on My Mind." After Scott finished, Seth shared that Ray Charles had performed that very song on the same piano. Seth, clearly impressed, then praised Scott's rendition, and Scott was so excited.

Despite Scott being seventeen, Josh and Brad treated him as an equal, including him in everything that went into production. They did producing, songwriting, arranging, composing, and postproduction, and Scott was with them, soaking it all up. Scott was frequently at their studio trying new things and creating music. Scott wrote on Josh's website: *Josh Goode is one of the most creative, talented, and kindest musicians I've ever worked with. We're always on the same page, and he brings so much creativity out of me. All my favorite songs I've written/recorded were ones I've worked on with him!*

Marty, along with her connections and experience, provided Scott with valuable exposure in the Dallas/Fort Worth area, securing him gigs at various venues and corporate events and giving him opportunities to sing the national anthem for the Mavericks. She took proactive steps to advance his career, including taking him to Los Angeles and arranging interviews with various record labels and even Disney, aiming to extend Scott's reach beyond the local scene.

As Scott started receiving more invitations, he needed to make an important decision. He had college dreams, with a special interest in one school in particular: USC. Despite his faith in Marty and the promising trajectory, Scott would choose USC. Marty gracefully released him from the management contract so that he could pursue college.

While parting ways with Marty was a difficult decision, she gave him an understanding of the complex nature of a career in music. The experience also helped him understand that it might be pragmatic for him to have a backup plan in case his childhood dream of singing all over the world didn't work out. So, along with the USC popular music degree, he decided that he would also pursue a degree in music business so that even if he didn't sing, he could still make a living as a part of the industry or get a foot in the door that way. At the time, I was relieved to see that he was thinking practically. However much we believed in him as his parents, we understood that some of the most talented, hardworking people still struggle to make a living in the music industry. *American Idol* had been a real lesson. Sometimes, talent isn't enough to ensure success. Would Scott be interesting enough to someone?

CHAPTER 7

"Mom, I'm Gay"

For many years, Scott didn't feel like he could openly be who he is.

He expressed himself musically, but he didn't share a big part of himself with me until he was seventeen. I was with him, on a long drive back from a piano lesson in Lewisville. It was like any ordinary day. We were just chatting about everyday things, when, a few miles from our house, he suddenly broke into tears. I was caught off guard and anxiously asked him what was wrong.

Scott paused for a moment, collected himself, and then he said to me, "Mom, I'm gay." Those words hung in the air momentarily. I was shocked—I had no idea, and I'd never really considered the possibility. He had always had girlfriends, and he had dated Kirstie for most of his sophomore year of high school.

I could see how difficult this conversation was for him, so I wanted to make sure that I responded the right way. In that vulnerable space, I told him that my love was unconditional and that being gay would not change how I felt about him in any way. He was still upset, but with my words, I hoped I could help him break free of the worry and complicated concerns he had no doubt been feeling for a long time. I had worries myself, as his mother, given what other gay men and women have had to face in our society in the late 2000s and prior. Looking back, I still don't know if it was the right thing to do, but I gently requested that Scott hold off on coming out to others until after he graduated from high school. I was concerned about bullying and discrimination, and I didn't want him to be ostracized by other high school kids. I asked him to wait until he went to college in Los Angeles, which I believed would be a more accepting environment. He shouldn't have to hide, I knew that, but I had so many fears on so many levels.

A few weeks later, Scott came home from a party. When I asked him how his evening went, he told me that it was good and bad. He arrived at the party, and a football player saw Scott and said, "Hey f**got, get lost, or I'll beat your ass." Fortunately, several kids at the party overheard him say this very homophobic slur and threat and told the football player to get out. Several people apologized to Scott, and the girl throwing the party said that that guy would never be welcome at her house again. Her response was comforting, but the incident was still unsettling, a validation of my deepest fears.

Even when Scott was set to move to California (a story still to come), I didn't really know of many openly gay singers at the time, and, as a mother, I worried that coming out might affect his future opportunities. After all, he was pursuing a career that would put him in the public eye. I hope he knows this thought was in the back of my mind when I cautioned him about telling too many people. We did our best to support him as he became and embraced his true self. But there are always, unfortunately, the practical considerations of a society that hasn't caught up to the reality of the varied and diverse identities people have. It's a balance between what is and what should be.

That car ride was a pivotal moment in our relationship, and I'm grateful that he was comfortable enough to have that conversation with me. After that, though, I had a new set of anxieties. What kinds of challenges would he face coming out with the pressure of societal expectations while also finding his authentic self and pursuing his passions? Would it all be too much?

A few weeks later, Scott came home and told us that the mother of a gay friend recommended a counselor. The counselor claimed to have once identified as gay but had gone through a process to become "straight." This was before we understood what exactly conversion therapy was. We were both curious, and I made the appointment.

As the day of the appointment approached, Scott had second thoughts and decided he no longer wanted to go. Despite his change of heart, I encouraged him to go, which I later regretted. We kept the appointment for no other reason than to hear the therapist's story. I was skeptical, but I wanted to see what the counselor had to say. I was still quite ignorant about it all, really. Reluctantly, Scott accompanied me to the session. The counselor shared his experiences and personal journey from identifying as gay to "embracing the heterosexual lifestyle."

The meeting started out very lighthearted, nothing ominous. The counselor seemed easygoing and joked that his wife appreciated his qualities that weren't traditionally masculine. He described himself as an excellent cook, an adept interior decorator, and the best-dressed husband. He also said he had more stereotypical male interests, like yard work, car repair, and various other tasks associated with stereotypical gender roles. I don't know why this part of the session stood out to me, other than I could relate to a wife appreciating someone good at so many things.

Then the meeting took a darker turn that upset Scott. The counselor brought up some of the religious aspects about homosexuality being a sin and the possibility of going to hell. The counselor also told Scott he would never be successful in music if he lived a gay lifestyle. Scott was getting annoyed and upset and was confident enough to respond that he believed that God wouldn't give him purpose and talents and then damn him for being gay. I was so impressed with his self-confidence—the way he stood up to this adult he just met and his belief in himself and his purpose.

Listening to the things coming out of the counselor's mouth that day was too much. The counselor discussed what he thought were some of the ugly "reasons" people became gay, like a bad relationship with the father or being molested at a young age, none of which applied to Scott, so we shut that down immediately. The session was a one-time experience, and we never returned. Scott cried for twenty-four hours afterward, and I was beyond freaked out because I had never seen Scott so sad in his life. I was so angry at myself for making that appointment. I knew this supposed therapy would not help Scott understand or accept himself, which is what I ultimately wanted.

Today, I understand better what conversion therapy is, and I would never want to put Scott through anything like that. I truly believe conversion therapy is horrific and should not exist. I am so incredibly proud of my son and son-in-law, who are so visibly queer and inspiring to LGBTQ+ people everywhere. I have witnessed countless times young men approaching Scott and thanking him for making them feel hopeful and showing them that it is possible to find love. He also told me he gets messages from young gay men and women almost daily.

Scott always ends the conversation by telling them, "You can be yourself and thrive!"

———

We would also face other spiritual conflicts after Scott came out. I am a very spiritual person and have always been a practicing Catholic, but I have been so disillusioned with the Catholic Church and its stance on homosexuality. It seems to have changed its stance a few times, but I recently read that their current stance is that it's not a sin to be gay. However, it is a sin to act on it. Scott could not get married in church, and the church would never recognize his marriage. This is something I so deeply disagree with and can't support, so it has deterred me from attending mass. Scott also no longer attends mass and hasn't for some time. All I can say is that I hope the church catches up someday.

———

After Scott came out, my journey to better understand him and other LGBTQ+ youth & young adults was shaped by several key events. In 2016, Pentatonix had just finished a concert in Dallas, and we were winding down after it. Scott had plans to meet some friends at a gay club in Dallas and invited Rick and me to go with him. Rick was tired and decided to opt out, but still buzzed from the excitement of their concert, I decided to join them. The night ended up being an unexpected emotional roller coaster. Scott introduced me to his friends, who seemed surprised that I willingly joined Scott at a gay club. I assumed it was due to my age, but that wasn't all it was.

As we shared stories, an awful reality became clear. Several of the young men there had been kicked out of their homes after coming out, abandoned by the very people who were meant to provide love and support. One by one, they recounted their ordeals. One young man spoke of nights spent alone in his car; another found refuge in a shelter. One told me that his parents said if he didn't lead a "straight" life, they wouldn't help him go to college. In the end, he could no longer be someone he wasn't. But in this adversity, there were touches of resilience. Friends rallied, offering places to stay and employment.

Hearing all of their stories was heartbreaking, and I can't comprehend how parents could treat their own children so badly. It tore me up that there were so many families broken because of discrimination. These men were the same children their parents loved and nurtured from the time they were born. Seeing their pain and strength left a mark on me, influencing me to commit to promoting inclusivity and acceptance for the LGBTQ+

community as an ally. No one should have to compromise themselves for family acceptance.

When it started to leak out back home that Scott was gay, some of the mothers I had known for years decided not to speak to me anymore. I considered these women friends, but suddenly, I was ostracized. One particular mother, whose son came out to her after Scott came out to me, blamed Scott for influencing him to be gay and me for enabling it. I told the young men back at that club in Dallas about that experience—how I felt like I was in a real-life adult version of the *Mean Girls* movie. We all laughed and had a group hug. I know it wasn't the same as what they had been through, but I felt such a new bond, not just with these lovely young men, but all LGBTQ+ people and their struggles after this night. It was the start of a new understanding for me.

———

A different movie helped put everything in perspective for me: *Love, Simon.* The movie is about a young gay man navigating the complexities of high school while grappling with his identity. Since Scott was not openly gay for most of his teenage life, this movie helped me understand the emotional weight he carried and what he went through.

The movie came out in 2018 after Pentatonix had already formed. It was a big deal, as this was one of the first films by a major Hollywood production that focused on a gay teenage romance. It meant so much to Scott to see a mainstream story so reflective of his high school experience. Scott and Mitch were so moved that they even rented a movie theater at our local mall and invited people from our hometown to watch it for free.

That's where I saw the movie for the first time, and it completely shifted my understanding of the struggles young gay people go through. I still get choked up when I think about the movie and what Scott must have gone through to keep his identity hidden from everyone. I hate that he experienced this inner turmoil while I saw him every day and had no idea. I was sobbing by the end of the movie. The film helped me connect to emotional struggles that were invisible to me, and I know it could do the same for others. I am grateful that more movies and shows are representing the diversity of the world. I hope that others, especially parents of LGBTQ+ children (but really everyone), will watch movies like these and help foster empathy, dismantle prejudice, and have a deeper understanding of those who have struggled silently.

———

Scott's ambition to build a career in the public eye also complicated his coming-out, as I had feared. In many industries, especially those with high visibility, like entertainment, sports, and media, there is significant pressure to maintain a particular image. Would audiences accept him for who he was? Or would he face discrimination and rejection? He realized that pretending to be straight was only bringing him pain, sadness, and anxiety. He did not want to live like that forever.

Scott went through a somewhat gradual coming-out process. He first told me and a few other close friends, Mitch Grassi being the first, and his sisters when he was seventeen, but when he attended USC, he did not hide his sexual orientation. However, when Pentatonix won *The Sing-Off*, he decided not to be public about his identity, worried about how it would affect the PTX brand.

Things changed in 2017 when he publicly came out in Pentatonix's "Imagine" music video. During the video, each member of the group took turns holding up signs that identified various aspects of their identities. Mitch Grassi, who is openly gay, was the first to hold up the LGBTQ+ sign, symbolizing the group's support for the community. He then passed the sign to Scott, who held it for a few seconds, clearly indicating his own identification as gay. This act was Scott's public coming-out, albeit subtle, marking the first time he had openly declared his sexuality to the world—a significant moment for Scott. He described the experience as liberating, feeling tremendous freedom and authenticity. Little did Scott know that the evening after shooting the "Imagine" music video would change his life forever. In a lot of ways, Scott was lucky. He had the support of his family and his friends. He came out on his own time and when he felt comfortable. While I wish now that we lived in a society where acceptance was assumed, we still don't. Everyone's story is unique, and each person must decide for themselves the *what* and *when* of safely disclosing their sexual identity. Scott's approach worked well for him, and we were lucky that acceptance has been more common.

I look forward to the day when LGTBQ+ people can freely be themselves without worrying about acceptance or rejection—or even worrying about coming out to begin with.

I am so proud of Scott for navigating the trials and tribulations of coming out with grace and facing societal pressures head-on while staying true to himself. In doing so, Scott not only carved out a successful career but also became a powerful advocate for LGBTQ+ rights.

———

I first heard about the Trevor Project when Pentatonix was on *The Sing-Off*. The show had each group select a charity, with a donation promised to the chosen organization of the winning group. Pentatonix had picked the Trevor Project. I didn't know anything about it, so I decided to research the organization.

I learned that the Trevor Project was founded in 1998 and named after the Academy Award–winning short film *Trevor*, which tells the story of a thirteen-year-old gay teenager who faces rejection and struggles with thoughts of suicide. It focuses on crisis intervention and suicide prevention among the LGBTQ+ youth. The organization offers resources for parents and educators to foster safe, accepting, and inclusive environments for all youth at home, schools, and colleges.

Whenever I give friends or family free tickets to Pentatonix shows, and they ask if they can donate to one of Scott's charities, I always recommend the Trevor Project. Scott has promoted and donated to the Trevor Project for years. One year, a very close friend of Scott's, Rich Handler, the CEO of Jefferies Investment Bank, had the firm donate $60K in Scott's name on their annual charity day.

Every year, thousands of minors are forced into homelessness by their families because of their sexual orientation. They provide counseling and many resources for LGBTQ+ youths. You can visit their website at https://www.thetrevorproject.org/. Unfortunately, *The Sing-Off* did not offer information about the charity, defining its LGBTQ+ focus, and, when some people found out, there was a backlash. It's just another reminder there is more work to be done.

You are not alone.

———

For all the parents out there whose child just told you that they're gay, I know you might be really confused. And that's okay. As long as you're leading with love, you don't have to fully understand at first. Did your child always date the opposite sex? Scott did, so I was surprised, to say the least. My next thoughts were fears and concerns, but those fears are nothing like the ones they have at that moment they are telling you. Scott was almost sobbing when he told me. I knew at that moment he had to know I unconditionally loved him, no matter what, as I had for seventeen years. I could sort through my confusion and questions later. If you shut them out or say anything hurtful, the damage could be significant to them and your relationship with them. I can't express enough that your child needs to feel your support and assurance that their sexual orientation does not change your love for them. I highly recommend the first words you say are, "I love you *so so so* much, and thank you for sharing something so personal and vulnerable with me."

The next important step is open and honest communication. Your child has to feel safe and in a nonjudgmental space where they can share their feelings and experiences. Over the next weeks or even years, you can ask questions. Scott had always dated girls, so I wanted to know when and how he knew. As for my silliest question—"Are you sure?"—you can probably skip that one.

I am still asking questions and always trying to understand. Years after he came out to me, I asked him if he knew he was gay when he was dating Kirstie. He said, "It was complicated. I was attracted to men [at that time], but I didn't want to be. I thought I was supposed to date girls."

He had planned to date girls, marry a girl, have a so-called normal life, and never tell anyone about his attraction to men. For several years, he kept this up, remaining silent.

Though the romantic relationship with Kirstie couldn't last, they remained very close friends. Scott felt safe with Kirstie and could be himself with her. Scott also felt safe with Mitch, and when Scott was seventeen, he came out to Mitch before anyone else. They dated privately for a short time.

Educate yourself about LGBTQ+ issues to better understand what your child might be going through. This knowledge will empower you to provide informed and compassionate support. However, don't go to a conversion therapist. The guilt and fear they try to instill are destructive. The Trevor Project might be a good place to start. Encourage your child to connect with LGBTQ+ communities where they can find acceptance. By embracing your child's identity and advocating for their well-being, you are fostering an environment where they can thrive and be their authentic self. Your acceptance and love can make a profound difference in their life.

Most importantly, make sure your child knows that you love them unconditionally and that their happiness is your top priority. It's all about love, after all.

Scan to listen to "Pray"—a special song by Scott Hoying and Toby Gad, released alongside this book. Enjoy!

CHAPTER 8

New Beginnings

The California dream, for Scott, began with the University of Southern California (USC), which caught his attention during his sophomore year of high school. He had learned about the USC Thornton School of Music and its undergraduate program in the music industry, which is recognized as one of the best in the nation. What truly captured his interest, however, was the addition of the Popular Music program, founded by Chris Sampson in 2009, the first program of its kind at a prestigious university. According to *Rolling Stone* magazine, USC Thornton's Popular Music program has made a significant impact in music and has a reputation as a cutting-edge department. It's become the site of one of Los Angeles's most productive new music scenes. And Sampson is at its center. A multifaceted educator, songwriter, producer, performer, and administrator, Sampson, as of this writing, serves as the vice dean for the Division of Contemporary Music at the USC Thornton School of Music. Many of his students have achieved remarkable success. They have had chart-topping hit songs, toured worldwide, secured coveted recording and publishing contracts, placed numerous songs in films and television, and are among the most subscribed musicians on YouTube. Additionally, many have won national television competitions and international songwriting competitions. Alumni also work in various parts of the music industry, including A&R (artists & repertoire), publishing, and administration.

———

When it came time to apply to USC, Scott completed all the standard forms and also had to submit a video of himself playing piano and singing. One of the songs he chose was Michael Bublé's "Feeling Good," which he felt demonstrated his musical range and expression. Aware of the competitive nature of admissions at USC and committed to going to college, Scott applied to other institutions, too, including Belmont University in Nashville, Berklee College of Music in Boston, John Hopkins University, the University of North Texas, and the University of Texas in Austin. Each application process brought its own set of challenges, requiring interviews and demonstrations of his musical abilities. Scott confidently navigated these interviews and earned invitations to perform in front of professors and admissions teams at many of the schools.

A few months later, several acceptance letters and scholarship offers started to trickle in. Scott received a full-ride offer from the University of North Texas, a partial scholarship from Berklee in Boston, and a partial scholarship from Belmont in Nashville.

However, Scott's dream finally came true when he received his acceptance letter from USC, just days after returning home from California, where he had performed live for the USC admission team. He wasted no time in responding and accepted USC's invitation to join the Thornton School of Music as a student, canceling the remaining interviews with the other colleges. It was an easy choice for Scott, who looked forward to the opportunity to immerse himself in the vibrant musical environment at USC.

Soon after, USC invited him back for further interviews for scholarships. They awarded him an academic dean's scholarship to help cover some of the costs. Unfortunately, music scholarships weren't available yet, but the vice dean of the music school let me know that there would be a chance for him to earn a music scholarship in the future. They hoped to offer them starting the next year. I was excited about that possibility because the two scholarships would alleviate most of the college's financial burden.

That burden intensified when Rick was laid off just as USC accepted Scott, leaving us scrambling for a solution to our financial dilemma. On top of our usual bills, we were now facing the future USC bills that would be coming down the road. The first thing I did was transition from a staff position to a full-time management position. I took on another job every other weekend to help make up some of the difference while Rick was looking for a new job. However, we knew that Scott would shortly be on his way to USC, a very expensive private college, and we had no clear plan how we were going to pay for it. We had faith that it would all work out. Rick found some consulting work, but it would be over a year before he got a full-time job.

But regardless, we were preparing to celebrate Scott's graduation from high school. As the baby in the family, Scott, up there accepting his diploma was everything to us—a mix of many emotions, marking the end of an era for our family. Lauren and Lindsay were all grown up, and Rick and I would soon have to adjust to being empty nesters. But we also felt the stark loss of no longer being a part of a community we'd been so deeply engaged in for twenty-six years through our kids. Although there was sadness knowing we would no longer be part of that familiar environment, we still shared in Scott's excitement for his next adventure in Los Angeles.

In August 2010, Scott would start at USC. Rick and I were excited about the prospect of driving him to Los Angeles and helping him get set up in the dorm. We were also looking forward to attending a local meet-and-greet on July 24 for newly accepted

Figure 8.1 Scott graduates from Martin High School. Author's family photo.

USC students and their parents who lived nearby. But we never made it to the event.

That morning, Rick was riding his motorcycle to a nearby jewelry store to resize a pearl ring he had given me for my birthday. Texas doesn't have laws requiring a helmet, and this particular day, he chose not to wear one. When he was on his way, a semi-truck turned in front of him, forcing Rick to make a split-second decision to lay down his bike to avoid hitting the truck head-on. The impact was devastating, and to this day, I still experience that sickening feeling in the pit of my stomach when I think about the call I received from the hospital telling me that there had been a bad accident. I was at work when I got the call. I asked the nurse if he was OK, and she responded that he was pretty broken. She then proceeded to tell me that after he laid the bike down, a car ran over him. I almost fainted, thinking the worst. Luckily, the car only ran over his left ankle, but I didn't know that then.

I left work at 11:00 a.m. and rushed to the hospital, trying to call family en route. When I arrived, I was told to sit in the waiting room, my mind racing. Suddenly, a minister approached, and a wave of dread washed over me. I broke down, thinking he was about to tell me my husband was gone. The minister quickly recognized my reaction and explained that David, my brother-in-law who was the head pastor of the hospital, had sent him to provide support until David and my family could come.

Rick was alive but in bad shape. He had a head injury, nine broken bones, damaged tendons, contusions, bruising, and severe road rash. A large round gash marred the left side of his head. All the injuries were on the left side since he laid the motorcycle down on that side.

Right when Scott and Lauren arrived at the hospital, both appearing stunned, the neurosurgeon came to the ER waiting room. He informed us that Rick had two clots in his brain that were causing significant swelling. He would need to perform surgery immediately and remove them, or Rick probably wouldn't survive. We all quickly told the surgeon to do whatever he needed to do. The staff allowed us to see Rick for a quick minute. He was unconscious, but we all told him we loved him, and within minutes they rushed him to the operating room. The fear and helplessness we felt were overwhelming, but we clung to the hope that the surgery would save his life.

After the brain surgery, multiple surgeries were scheduled to address the extensive damage to his left ankle, shoulder, and scapula. The first night in the hospital at around midnight, I was woken up by Rick screaming out in pain. I jumped off the couch, and two doctors were standing over him trying to put his ankle bones back into place. Two days later, he had surgery to have pins placed in his ankle. He had a collapsed lung, and a tube was placed in his chest as well.

Our daughter Lindsay, who is in the navy, was deployed overseas at the time. We sent a Red Cross message to see if she could come home. We conveyed the seriousness of the situation without giving her all the details, not wanting to upset her. However, she noticed a note indicating that her leave was to be approved due to her father having life expectancy issues. She suspected that either I wasn't telling her the whole truth or her commander wanted to ensure her leave was approved. She made it home two days later and was able to stay for two weeks, not leaving until Rick was stable.

Rick spent ten days in the ICU. I didn't leave his side for five days, sleeping on a narrow couch. Scott was still living at home and brought me the necessities I needed. On the fifth day, Rick was stable, so I could go home and shower. After five more days, he was transferred out of the ICU to a regular room. He then spent ten days in a rehab facility. Fortunately, Rick was transferred to the facility where I was Director of Rehab. He was given constant attention as my therapists worked with him, which included physical therapy, occupational therapy, and speech therapy.

He then came home, and we thought the worst was over. But it was not. He still had to have shoulder surgery because he was unable to move it. The surgery went well, but he got an infection. He had to have a home health nurse come twice a day for IV antibiotics. He then had to return to the hospital for another shoulder surgery and have it repaired again.

Over the next several months he had to sleep in a recliner, because sleeping flat was too painful. He was in a wheelchair for six weeks. After that, he transitioned to a walker, and a month later, he could use crutches. He still had to wear a boot for several months and eventually used a cane. I gave him home health therapy and his healing journey demanded immense strength and patience for both of us.

While Rick was home, and on the road to recovery he wrote the following story as memories started to return:

I was now above my motorcycle watching a white tractor-trailer turning left into my pathway. I didn't see how I could miss the truck, but in my new state of mind, I did. Everything was different though. I was no longer riding the bike but in another place that I can't describe. It was beyond words and it was pure bliss. I had never felt more wonderful. But all I could think of was Where am I and what is happening? I had Connie's ring in my pocket and I had to get to the jewelers to get it resized. Where I was I did not know, but it was very pleasant. I had strong feelings of complete serenity, security, and warmth. I was comfortable, happy, and surrounded by love. I had an overwhelming sense that everything was perfect. There was no pain. In fact, I remember trying to recall how long it had been when I felt no pain at all. The feeling was utter bliss. Still, I was confused and wanted to understand. I remained in this state for a while. How long? I don't know, since time seemed to have been suspended. I remember wanting to go back to my old reality to finish the ring errand, and fighting to do so. Suddenly I woke up briefly inside an ambulance with two EMTs working on me. I could hear the siren, and I could feel the movement of the vehicle. Now I felt terrible pain but could not tell what hurt. My head was spinning. I recall speaking with the EMT. I tried to give him Connie's cell number, but I don't know if he heard or understood me. I tried to move but could not do so. I realized that I had been in an accident and that things were very bad.

*I did not, however, feel any fear that I might die, but I did
mentally resign myself to the fact that I had no control. I was
in the hands and care of God and others.*

Since the accident, Rick has said several times that he no longer
fears death. He doesn't necessarily want to die anytime soon
because of the love he has for his family, but he knows when he
does go, it's going to be peaceful.

Rick wasn't able to accompany Scott on his move to USC. He
was disappointed but determined to be well enough to visit during
parents' weekend in October. I flew out with Scott to Los Angeles
and moved him into his dorm, which ended up being a converted
Ritz Hotel due to a shortage of dorm rooms (no complaints about
that here). It's funny how the good can happen alongside the bad.
Scott was at the start of a new exciting adventure just as our family
was experiencing one of our biggest challenges to date.

Despite still needing his boot and cane, Rick was able to
attend USC's parents' weekend in October. The weekend was
packed with activities. On the first day, Scott gave us a cam-
pus tour, and we sat in on one of Scott's classes, which Chris
Sampson taught. We were so impressed by his interaction with
his students. After that class, I fully understood Scott's admiration for him and enthusiasm for his teaching. The second day
revolved around a football game. It started with tailgating, with
lunch provided before the big game at the Coliseum. Postgame,
we joined in on after-parties and treated Scott to dinner. Seeing
him so content filled us with joy.

———

Scott loved USC as much as he thought he would. The proximity
to stardom was an unexpected bonus, as many celebrities served
as teachers or guest speakers. It didn't take long for Scott to
find his footing in classes and the world of collegiate a cappella
with USC's SoCal VoCals, which, over the years, has won five

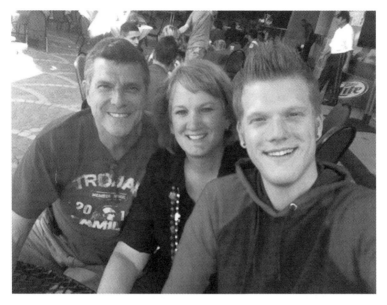

Figure 8.2   Scott, Mom, and Dad at USC's parents weekend. Author's family photo.

International Championship of Collegiate A Cappella (ICCA) titles and released eight studio albums to date. They have also performed at prestigious venues like Carnegie Hall and the Lincoln Center. He had to audition for the group and, considering their accomplishments, this was no easy feat. There were only a few spots open, so the competition was fierce. Two weeks into the school year, I received a phone call from Scott. He phoned me with news of his acceptance. I could hear the joy and excitement in his voice. He had never dreamed of being in an a cappella group. Yet he was ready when the discovery and opportunity arose, and he dove in deep. Along with a fraternity for performance art students that he joined, SoCal VoCals gave him a community of musical friends, a home away from home. Scott loved performing at venues with SoCal VoCals and in competitions against other colleges, which wasn't surprising given his extensive participation in contests over the years. Pitted against other groups, his friends in SoCal VoCals bonded even more. The group also had retreats and team-building activities. The camaraderie within the group reminded me of his high school choir days when music was not just a performance but a shared passion. Scott found himself surrounded by many kindred spirits. It was official: Scott was hooked on a cappella for life! ♪

During the summer, Scott was able to stay in the SoCal VoCal housing, which is the only reason why he was able to stay in Los Angeles and try out for *The Sing-Off*. As Scott would say, he was "living his best life."

Scott found so much inspiration in the industry professionals around him at USC, particularly the chance to learn songwriting, music theory, genre styles like R&B, and even drumming from these amazing talented professionals. The school also encouraged practical application by placing students in bands and having them collaborate and perform with talented peers like Lara Thompson (daughter of Tom Johnston, the lead singer of the Doobie Brothers), Rozzi Crane, and so many more.

In fact, Scott was placed in a band with drummer Mac Sinese (Gary Sinese's son). When Scott told me about playing with Mac, I was stunned, since Gary Sinese was a major celebrity crush of mine. A few years later at the CMAs, I ended up sitting right next to Mac and Gary and almost had a heart attack. Scott was sitting in front of me, and he leaned over, remembering what I had told him and begged me to please not ask for a selfie. I didn't, but I may have snuck a picture of Gary during the show. And, after the show, I had the chance to chat with both Gary and Mac, and they were both incredibly nice and humble.

Randomly, Rick, who was seated about ten rows back, was with another celebrity crush of mine—Harry Connick Jr. (*I can hear you judging me; stop.*) The sight of the two of them, engaged in conversation, was a surreal moment in an already unforgettable evening.

While writing this book, I was deeply saddened to learn that Mac Sinese died of a rare form of cancer in January 2024. I want to extend my deepest sympathies to his family and loved ones.

———

Scott was in his freshman year at USC when he auditioned for the first season of *The Voice*. Like *American Idol*, he made it through rounds of tryouts and got to the very end. But, here he was told he'd made the show! He was ecstatic; it was finally happening. Then, just a day before he was supposed to move to the contestants' hotel, he got a call from the casting director.

He had been cut from the competition.

They told Scott that they decided to go with a different tall, blond contestant instead. Scott was understandably upset (not as much as I was), but, in Scott's way, he shrugged it off and said to me, "You know what, Mom? When one door closes, another one opens." He moved on and continued his studies at USC.

Thirteen years after Scott's disappointment with *The Voice*, a similar experience happened to his sister, Lauren. She also auditioned for the show and enjoyed four weeks at the contestants' hotel. However, right after her dress rehearsal and a couple of days before her blind audition, she was unexpectedly cut from the lineup. Despite the setback, Lauren still is glad she did it. To her, those four weeks were like a music camp, surrounded by like-minded people who loved singing as much as she did. She fondly remembers the kindness of everyone involved in the show and the incredible talent of the contestants. She also made lifelong friends she continues to root for as they continue their journeys. In fact, in May 2024, Lauren and I went to the finals to support her friends who made it to the final five. Bryan Olesen, who was in the final five of season 25, got us our tickets to the finals. We had great seats and if you look really closely, you can see us for a second.

Scott, who later had the opportunity to perform on *The Voice* with PTX, also commented on the kindness of everyone involved with the show. We know there is an abundance of talented people in the world, and you have to make the show really interesting to maintain viewership. It still stings, though, to get so close and get cut at the last minute, right before going on national TV.

Not even two weeks after getting cut from *The Voice*, Scott first heard about upcoming auditions for an a cappella show called *The Sing-Off* through SoCal VoCals. He had a chance meeting with Ben Bram, a USC graduate, at an alumni party. During that conversation, Ben encouraged Scott to form a group and audition for the show. Scott, even though he was fresh off the disappointment from *The Voice*, did not hesitate. He just had to get together at least five people and come up with a name. It's wild to think that if *The Voice* had ended up picking him instead of the other "tall, blond one," then Pentatonix might never have happened.

CHAPTER 9

The Rise of Pentatonix

When Scott told me about *The Sing-Off,* I was a little skeptical. After everything with *American Idol* and *The Voice,* I had reservations about reality TV competition shows. I'm not knocking them, though. The disappointments he dealt with were an important step in his growth as an artist and his understanding of how things work behind the scenes. He would later meet so many wonderful and talented people from those shows, including Kelly Clarkson and Randy Jackson, both of *American Idol,* who have become good friends and collaborators. Pentatonix even opened for Kelly during one of her tours, and she was on one of Pentatonix's TV Christmas specials. Scott and Kelly were also nominated for an Emmy in 2021 for a song they wrote on her show, "Cabana Boy Troy." Still, reality television can be tough, and I didn't want him going through the roller coaster of emotions and the endless uncertainty all over again. I couldn't shake the feeling of "not another one."

I kept my reservations to myself, supporting Scott as I always did, but I wasn't the only one with reservations. To form his group for *The Sing-Off,* Scott reached out to his friends from "The Trio": Kirstie Maldonado, who was attending Oklahoma University, and Mitch Grassi, who was a senior in high school getting ready to graduate. Mitch's dad was far from thrilled about his son auditioning for a reality show. Mitch would have to miss his high school graduation with no promise of making it past the audition. Mitch's dad repeatedly said no. But when he learned that Scott was organizing it and Kirstie was on board, he finally gave in. Scott had the Trio back together again. But they still needed two more members. And so the search for a beatboxer and a bass began.

———

Scott found a bass pretty quickly thanks to Ben Bram, who originally encouraged Scott to try out for the competition. He was a well-connected figure in the world of music and a cappella. He had a musician in mind, and he wanted Scott to meet him. Ben said that the bass he was recommending had a background in classical training and accolades from ICCA competitions: Avi Kaplan.

Ben assured Scott that Avi would enhance the group. Scott watched some videos of Avi and was very impressed. Scott wanted to meet up as soon as possible. The first thing Avi said was that he usually didn't like to do reality shows. However, he had seen the viral video of the Trio, and he was so enthralled that he was open to joining the group. Avi's skills were impressive, and Scott offered Avi a spot in the band. Avi gladly accepted. One down, one more to go.

———

To find a beatboxer, he and Ben Bram decided to get help from YouTube. They went to the computer, and Scott typed in the keyword "beatboxers" just to see what they could find. Among the videos, one really stood out to him. Kevin Olusola was beatboxing while playing "Julie-O" on the cello. The video had recently gone viral, and Scott was obsessed. He quickly messaged Kevin through YouTube, hoping to persuade him to audition for *The Sing-Off* alongside their group. It seemed like a long shot because everyone was posting about him, from big press outlets to Justin Timberlake.

At first, Kevin didn't seem interested. He was finishing pre-med at Yale and getting ready to start medical school. Scott didn't have much hope, so they tried a few other beatboxers that were local. They auditioned a kid named Moonsoo, who was insanely talented. However, when the group sang with him, it wasn't a fit—they couldn't stay in sync. Next, they considered another talented beatboxer called Beats. He was most likely going to be the fifth member, but then, right before the audition, Kevin got back to Scott and told him that he had graduated and he was down to audition with them. Scott felt he was perfect for the group, and immediately stopped his search. He and Ben pooled their money and bought Kevin a ticket, bringing him from the East Coast to LA. Scott and Kirstie picked Kevin up the day before the audition. Scott told me, "It's such a wild thing to think about." Life, or at least Scott's life, was full of serendipitous moments. A simple search on YouTube yielded the fifth member!

Kevin has been asked many times, especially in interviews, what his parents said when he told them that he was going to be a beatboxer rather than a doctor. Kevin always laughed at this question but I don't remember if he's ever answered it.

———

Each person in the group has a distinctive voice and style with diverse musical backgrounds and vocal capabilities, and all five (six, including Matt, who would later replace Avi) are immensely talented.

- Scott primarily sings the baritone role within the group, though he occasionally steps in as a bass or tenor when needed. A highly skilled pianist, Scott sometimes showcases his talent on the piano too. Scott is also heavily involved in arranging the group's music, though he still has time for his solo ventures. He released a solo album, *Parallel*, in July 2023.

- Mitch, the group's tenor, has also played the piano since age five. Beyond his vocal duties, Mitch has a passion for electropop music and released an EP, *Roses*, in August 2021. He goes by the name of Messer for his solo projects.

- Kirstie is the mezzo-soprano/alto of the group and has a love for acting and musical theater. This was her original goal when she attended college. In July 2017, Kirstie released a solo album called *Love*. She also starred in *Kinky Boots* on Broadway in 2018, achieving one of her dreams. She starred alongside David Cook and Wayne Brady.

- Kevin, the beatboxer, is a classical music enthusiast and a master of the cello, which he can play while beatboxing. He calls it "celloboxing." It is quite a treat to hear him performing this talent at concerts, and occasionally, you will hear him sing tenor on songs. Kevin released an EP titled *The Renegade EP*.

- Avi has a rich deep bass voice and would occasionally sing baritone. He also has a unique talent and can sing two different notes simultaneously: a bass note and a whistle-like note, called an "overtone." He would do this trick occasionally during concerts. In 2017 Avi left the group to pursue a solo career and was replaced by Matt Sallee that same year.

- Matt has a huge range from low bass notes—his primary role with PTX—to high falsetto notes. He has a lovable charisma, and a passion for harmony whether it be in choir, church, or Pentatonix. He also is a great drummer and frequently drums in PTX shows. Ben Bram had a hand in finding Matt for the group. When Matt auditioned in 2017, he already had all the bass parts memorized for all Pentatonix songs.

These dynamic artists lived in different parts of the country prior to the audition. Due to conflicting schedules—Kirstie was still in school at Oklahoma University, Mitch was finishing high school, and Kevin was flying out—the only available rehearsal day was June 4. The audition was on June 5. They weren't able to test out their chemistry or see how they sounded together until a day before the audition, when Kevin arrived from the East Coast. With limited time, the group decided to expand on what the Trio had already done in high school: Lady Gaga's hit song, "Telephone." Scott sent arrangements to Kevin and Avi who, despite the time crunch, were able to put together their parts.

They met at the SoCal Vocal house at USC, where Scott was living at the time. There were eight people living there, and it was a typical frat house (though perhaps a bit more creative): kind of messy, people coming and going frequently. Despite the chaos, it was the only place they could find to rehearse. And thank goodness it wasn't a week later. All the residents had to move out for a couple of days so that Steve Carell could shoot a scene in Scott's bathtub for the movie *Seeking a Friend for the End of the World*. How crazy is that?

Kevin's flight was coming in late, so they couldn't meet until the evening. They only had three hours to rehearse, and it was down to the wire. When they all arrived, they decided to start by just singing through the entire song of "Telephone" to get a feel for their sound. Scott couldn't believe the harmonious sound that was coming out of the group. They spent the next three hours rehearsing it over and over to refine it and make their rendition of "Telephone" as perfect as possible. They briefly rehearsed two other songs, "Sweet Dreams" and "Rolling in the Deep," to make sure they had something ready in case they were asked to do more songs. After the rehearsal, Kirstie and Mitch stayed in Scott's room while Kevin stayed at Avi's.

Late that evening (very late my time), Scott excitedly called me, "Mom, our chemistry is incredible, I think we have something really special." My concern about yet another reality TV attempt was starting to disappear. Scott would never have said that if it wasn't true.

I find it interesting that in a later interview on the show with Sara Bareilles, she stated, "I think they're innovators, pushing boundaries in the right ways; they have incredible chemistry." Scott said something similar to me on that call.

The next morning they arrived at a studio in Burbank, where auditions were being held. There were hundreds of people, maybe even a thousand, Scott told me, making up many groups—anywhere from eight to fifteen singers in each—all eager to compete on the show. As the smallest group, with only five members, they felt a bit nervous, concerned that their sound might not be big enough compared to these larger groups.

Still, they were ready when they were called up to sing about midday. They thought "Telephone" was a strong song and felt good about the performance. When they finished, the judges requested another song and then another one. They were fairly confident about "Sweet Dreams" and "Rolling in the Deep" since they had more time to rehearse them that morning and they nailed those too. But then the judges wanted one more and the group hadn't prepared for that.

Fortunately, Scott, Kirstie, and Mitch knew the song "Fireworks" because they had arranged it in high school. The group had not rehearsed it at all, though, and Scott, Kirstie, and Mitch hadn't sung it in over a year. They put on a confident front and started singing "Fireworks," with their whole heart. Kevin and Avi listened for a moment and joined in, improvising their parts on the fly. Scott said the judges were blown away, and that's the moment Scott thought they just might make it on the show. The on-the-spot thinking and creativity alone demonstrated some amazing talent. The judges didn't know the backstory, but hopefully, the sound would be enough.

Just a few hours after all of the excitement of the audition, the group went to Olive Garden for dinner. They all felt good about

Figure 9.1 PTX auditions for *The Sing-Off*. Author's family photo.

the audition but were still unsure if they would be chosen. During dinner, Scott received a phone call from the casting director. They had made it onto the show! The casting director gave some information and provided the dates they needed to be available. Scott tried to focus enough to remember and to write down everything he was hearing. They were shocked to find out that early but very relieved they didn't have to wait in anticipation for weeks. Their talent, hard work, and adaptability had paid off. But there was still one issue: They needed a name.

Scott suggested that since there were five of them, they could play on the musical scale built around five notes, the pentatonic scale. He liked the idea of using an "x" instead of a "cs" to make it "cooler": Pentatonix. A network executive, however, thought the name was hard to spell, hard to say, and hard to remember. He suggested they try different names, so they came up with several alternatives like "Perfect Fifth," "Plead the Fifth," and even "Fifth Harmony." The executive didn't like those either. They kept trying different names up until the day they shot the first episode, ultimately sticking with Pentatonix. This name also eventually led to the frequently used acronym PTX.

Taping for the competition was set to begin, so all five of them and other contestants moved to the Doubletree Hotel for months of weekly competitions. There were sixteen groups in the competition, and there would be weekly eliminations. The show ran for eleven episodes, first airing on September 19, 2011, and concluding with the live finale on November 28, 2011.

Every Friday night from July through early September, they taped a show, creating a routine that became a roller coaster of nerves and excitement. I worked until noon each Friday, rushed to the airport, and boarded a plane to LA. The show was taped in Century City each week. I would take an Uber to the studio and have an early dinner nearby at the Backstage Bar and Grill. Being a creature of habit and superstition, I would have chicken wings and a beer to settle my nerves. I never changed my routine or the food I ate. I would then join the line at 4:30 p.m. to secure a seat for the show.

After the show, sometimes as late as 2:00 a.m., I'd call Rick to share whether the group had made it through. Rick was caught up in his own work commitments and travel and was only able to join a few times. He was still getting settled in his new job and didn't want to push for too much time off.

The very first show, though, Rick was with me in line for the taping. As we waited, we started talking to the girl next to us and asked her if she knew someone in the competition. Her response was, "Yes, my brother is in the group Pentatonix." It was Avi's sister, Esther Kaplan.

———

Every single week, Scott would start rehearsal by asking the band, "How can we make this arrangement really special, creative, and memorable?"

He says that this mindset stemmed from the motorcycle trip to Alaska he took with his dad. Every time they took a picture, Rick would ask, "How can we make this picture creative?"

The question resulted in several little flairs they added to the songs, including music-skipping in "Video Killed the Radio Star." Before the bridge of "Dog Days Are Over," there was supposed to be a beat or two of silence, but the day before the performance, Scott suggested to Mitch that he just hold it through. Mitch crushed it, and that ended up being such a phenomenal moment. They also added gunshot sounds in "Born to Be Wild," among other creative touches. Those little flairs were well received, and he saw that bold creative risks can pay off.

Of course, there was plenty of drama along the way, especially by the time they made it to the finals. One week, Kristin was really sick, but fortunately, she still had a voice and managed to push through. There was an occasional panic attack, especially when they had to change their song at the last minute. Like any family, there were disagreements and creative differences. The rehearsals began in the early morning and went late into the evening. The schedule wore on them, but they all gave it everything they had. The closer they got to reaching the finals, the more they gave.

For Scott, the most dramatic moment was during the final taped show. That day, Scott called to tell me he had a severe case of laryngitis: he could barely talk and didn't think he'd be able to perform. This was the last taped show of the competition, and it was meant to determine the winner via television audience votes. He was drinking hot tea and doing steaming treatments, but nothing seemed to help. Scott's voice was in jeopardy, and he was beside himself.

An hour before the performance, they called in a doctor to see Scott on set. Behind a flimsy curtain right by the stage, the doctor gave him a shot in the behind and said you should be good to go. I was in the audience at this point and had no idea what was going on or how he was feeling. Would he come out onstage, barely able to sing? I just didn't know, and I was praying.

Scott must have been very stressed and still sick when he took the stage, but you couldn't tell. It was obvious to the audience and viewers that Scott was giving it everything he could, especially near the end when he had to sing the most powerful notes. I still can't believe he pushed through, and the song was amazing. It's one of my favorite performances from the show, and I still get chills whenever I go back and listen to it.

Fortunately, all five were able to perform every week despite illness and other issues. Since only five were in the group—unlike most of their competitors, who had eight to fifteen members— they all had to do their part, or the song would not work. Scott credits *The Sing-Off* with significantly boosting his work ethic, which surprised me, considering the amount of work he had always put into his projects. His work ethic really wasn't too shabby to begin with. ♪

———————

Pentatonix made it to the live finale when the winner would be announced. Our whole family attended; Lindsay even flew in from England, where she was stationed. We went to dinner the night before, except for Scott, due to long rehearsal days before the finale. We made a toast to an absent Scott and cheered on Pentatonix. It was such an emotional time with my grown children in such wildly different places in life but all of us there together, thanks to music.

The atmosphere at the live finale was electric, buzzing with excitement and filled with anticipation as fans eagerly awaited the big announcement. Three amazingly talented groups were in the finals—Dartmouth Aires, Urban Method, and Pentatonix. They emerged out of sixteen groups. The competition was intense all season, and we were all on the edge of our seats, anticipating the winner's coronation. The venue was quite big and had bleacher-like seating in a "U" shape with a table and chairs in the middle of them. We were at the very top of the bleachers, about midway. I could hardly breathe because I was so nervous.

The finale featured many performances, with the judges and Nick Lachey joining the contestants on stage. Pentatonix, along with Nick, delivered a rendition of "Give Me Just One Night (Una Noche)" by 98 Degrees, the boy band that included Nick. Following that, Pentatonix performed "Without You," which had a bit of drama. Scott recounts, "The monitors were *so* loud that we couldn't tell what note we were given at the beginning of the song. I came in on a random key, and we had to scramble to find our footing. It was such a huge bummer."

The other finalists and judges also performed, though I honestly can't remember much about them except for Pentatonix's performance. I was so nervous I could barely think straight.

As the tension peaked, the three finalists were ushered onto the stage. Shawn Stockman commended Urban Method for their determination and resilience, expressing his pride in their journey. Sara Bareilles then turned her attention to the Dartmouth Aires, praising their commanding presence and urging them to channel their energy with focus, hopefully on Broadway stages. Then Ben Folds told Pentatonix they had the potential to take a cappella into the mainstream. He said to write with the best writers and producers in the business and to have a good time. With a blend of encouragement and humor, he told them to stay in the Knights Inn when they are on tour because it's cheap.

Following the individual acknowledgments, Nick Lachey carefully built anticipation, showcasing each group before announcing the third-place team: Urban Method. They performed their swan song: a heartfelt rendition of "Coming Home." Urban Method bid farewell, and the spotlight shifted to Dartmouth Aires and Pentatonix.

After showcasing the TV packages for Dartmouth Aires and then Pentatonix, the moment of truth arrived. Anticipation was thick in the air. The most agonizing part was the very long pause—close to one minute, which felt like days—before the winner was declared. I felt the urge to scream building within me until finally, he stated . . .

"America has voted, and the group that has won *The Sing-Off* is . . . Pentatonix!"

The crowd erupted with cheers and applause. Rick had to steady me as I lost my balance in my excitement, in danger of tumbling off the back of the bleachers where we were standing. The groups were all hugging and crying, and confetti was everywhere. Pentatonix was just crowned the third-season winner of *The Sing-Off*!

Pentatonix then finished the show singing "Eye of the Tiger," and it was settled: They were the champions! It was such a thrilling night, reflecting the culmination of not only sixteen weeks of dedication, uncertainty, and, ultimately, triumph, but also a dream come true for all of them.

Reflecting on Scott's journey, including auditions for *American Idol* three times, *The Voice* disappointment, *AGT*, and *Star Search*, along with releasing albums, voice lessons, piano lessons, and countless challenges, I couldn't help but cry, thinking, "They did it! Success!"

Resilience is a powerful thing.

———

After the live finale, our family was invited to an after-party to celebrate. It took place at a swanky Hollywood bar called Rush. The atmosphere was alive with optimism about the future. The guest list included contestants, judges, families, and friends. Lindsay was starstruck when she met one of her favorite singers, Ben Folds. For the next several days, she kept repeating in astonishment what had happened: She had met Ben Folds! It's probably similar to how I felt meeting Kenny Loggins. We also talked with Shawn Stockman, Sara Bareilles, and the host, Nick Lachey. Being a bit starstruck myself, I tried not to ask dumb questions, but I probably did. People say that there are no stupid

Figure 9.2 PTX wins *The Sing-Off*. Author's family photo.

questions, but those people probably never asked Nick Lachey where he gets his T-shirts.

We took numerous pictures with the judges and the host, and I hope we didn't embarrass Scott. There were hundreds of people in attendance, with complimentary food and drinks for all. The judges and Nick Lachey were so friendly and approachable. They really seemed to think Pentatonix had something truly special, and it was so much fun talking to them about PTX's future.

After that, many of us met at the DoubleTree, where all of the contestants had stayed for months. It was a beautiful hotel. We all stayed up until the wee hours of the morning, mostly reliving the excitement of the whole season and talking about what might come next. No one wanted the evening to end.

I am so grateful that my entire family had the opportunity to be a part of such a magical night. It wasn't just the competition; it was about experiencing genuine joy and happiness for Scott. That night will always feel like the realization of a dream turned into reality, with all of us there to witness the magic.

Figure 9.3 After-party at the Rush bar. Author's family photos.

I'm not sure why we booked early-morning flights the next day, but both Rick and I managed to sleep through the alarm clock. We finally woke up with Lauren pounding on our door. From there, it was a bit like the morning scene from *Home Alone*, minus the cop with a gold tooth—everyone trying to get everything together and rush to the airport in record time. Despite the chaos, we caught our flight, and now we look back and laugh about the whole ordeal.

Scott couldn't return home with us because PTX was performing in an NBC TV Christmas special the following week. That meant more rehearsals and long days for them, but I'm pretty sure they didn't mind. They sang Justin Bieber's "Mistletoe." They also performed alongside past winners and other stars.

We could not attend the special, but we watched it on TV with friends and family. This appearance would be the first of many Christmas specials they would do, and they would go on to become known for their Christmas music.

I can't help but feel a bit guilty that I ever doubted Scott's interest in another reality show. The irony is that I never once questioned Scott when he tried out for the other shows, only *The Sing-Off*—the one that brought him a real career start. Scott was always determined to say yes to everything that crossed his path, to make sure he didn't overlook any potential opportunity. And in this case, I'm so glad he has that drive in him. He had a determination that would lead him to victory, even when there were always other tall, blond ones.

Chapter 10

Finding Solid Footing in the Music Biz

After *The Sing-Off*, Scott made the difficult decision to end his time at USC. He wanted to put his all into Pentatonix, and returning to USC for his sophomore year would hinder his ability to do that. Scott kept in close contact with Chris Sampson, keeping him updated on Pentatonix's progress during the tapings, so it wasn't a complete surprise. Chris gave Scott an exceptional level of understanding and support during this time, assuring him that he would always be welcomed back at USC. I will always be grateful for the supportive nature of Chris and the USC music program and their genuine investment in the success and well-being of each student.

Despite Scott's brief tenure at USC, he is still grateful for the wealth of knowledge he gained during his time there. The opportunity to learn from renowned musicians through master classes and meeting industry giants left a lasting impression. It was life-changing. Scott told me there was an inside joke among the students: "If you graduated, you failed." The joke referred to the countless connections at USC, suggesting that with so many opportunities available, you wouldn't need to stay until graduation to succeed.

Several opportunities arose from attending USC in just that one year. Pentatonix wouldn't have been possible if he didn't go to USC, his musical's first workshop was funded by a USC SoCal Vocal alumni, and he had a podcast with Rozzi Crane, an up-and-coming artist with whom Scott has collaborated on many projects. With Pentatonix's third-season win of *The Sing-Off*, they won a record deal from Epic Records and $40,000 each. Everyone in the group moved to Los Angeles and lived in three apartments near the iconic Grove neighborhood.

Dr. Bill Dorfman, known for being the dentist for the stars, was a big help in getting them settled. He met the group at *The Sing-Off* after-party. He was Nick Lachey's dentist and attended the show and after-party as a guest of Nick's after fixing Nick's chipped tooth that day. Bill was involved in some makeover and medical TV shows, too, and offered to help Pentatonix find apartments, along with furniture. He also connected them with a lawyer to navigate the complexities of music industry contracts and, of course, became their dentist. His company, Zoom, would help finance one of their first music videos, "Starships."

Life was falling into place for the ensemble, and they started brainstorming and preparing for their new life as recording artists in Los Angeles. They acquired a manager, JK, who got the ball rolling for touring and recording albums. In the first few weeks, they got gigs in Florida, New York, and LA, and interviews everywhere. Rick and I resumed our life back home, returning to work as usual. Scott, incredibly happy, called frequently to keep us updated on all the exciting events unfolding. He was also incredibly busy, but that's how he liked it. Unfortunately, the good times didn't last long.

Just a few weeks after winning *The Sing-Off*, Epic Records dropped them from their label. Epic had just made major staff changes, including a new CEO, L. A. Reid. PTX had a meeting scheduled with him, but he didn't show up for the meeting. His second-in-command did, and she laughed in their faces and said they didn't have the time or money to take a risk on them. PTX were shocked and heartbroken. Scott tried fervently to persuade her otherwise, attempting to convince her of their potential.

She ended up offering to keep them under the Epic label but only if they would add instruments. Epic didn't think a cappella could go mainstream, and it just didn't know what to do with them. All five agreed that staying a cappella was nonnegotiable. They refused the compromise and were let go from the contract, which wasn't particularly favorable to them anyway. The search for another label began.

At the time, the quick change in fortune was devastating, especially in light of the sacrifices all the members made in their move to Los Angeles. Scott left USC; Kirstie left Oklahoma University, where she was studying music theater on a full-ride scholarship; and Mitch left behind his college ambitions. When Scott called, Mitch had been trying to decide between OU and SMU—both had offered full rides. Kevin had opted out of medical school after graduating premed from Yale, and Avi had abandoned his own plans after completing his education at Mt. San Antonio College, where he studied opera and choral music. They were not only a musically talented group but they also all had other options, which were very good options.

Despite losing the label deal, no one wanted to give up and return to their previous lives, and it ended up being a positive moment in their career. In the music industry, contracts can significantly impact an artist's path. The contract with Epic Records was very restrictive and limited them creatively and financially. Being able to get out of that contract opened doors for them to explore new opportunities and to make creative decisions that aligned better with their vision of what Pentatonix could be.

———

In their next move, Pentatonix turned to the platform that would play a crucial role for them: YouTube. Hoping to grow the fan base they had gained from *The Sing-Off*, the group began posting videos on their YouTube channel. They covered popular songs like "Somebody That I Used to Know," "We Are Young," and created innovative mash-ups like the "Evolution of Music," and Scott's favorite, "The Evolution of Beyoncé." That caught the attention of Ellen Degeneres, who invited them to come on the show and perform it.

The set was simple—they would sit on a couch or just stand in a room.

A lot of these low-budget, informal videos would not have been allowed under their previous contract. Their strategy ended up being a very successful one. They attracted many viewers to their YouTube channel, possibly more than from *The Sing-Off*. And every time they gained another thousand subscribers, we marked the occasion with an online celebration, or "Penta Party." Family, friends, and fans all would join online to chat and celebrate together.

At the same time that they started posting YouTube videos, PTX's management was trying to find them another label, but every major label said, "No, not interested." Finally, a small label called Madison Gate Records said yes in January 2012. Even though the label only had three employees and its specialty was soundtracks for movies, TV shows, and other entertainment media, they believed in Pentatonix and gave them a chance. Pentatonix did several EPs under the Madison Gate label, and they were received well. Their debut *EP PTX, Volume I* was released in 2012 and charted number fourteen on the *Billboard* 200. That was followed by their holiday release *PTXmas* that same year, which charted number four on *Billboard*'s Holiday chart. The turning point was Pentatonix's third release, *PTX Vol. II*, debuting at number one on *Billboard*'s Independent Albums chart and number ten on the *Billboard* 200 in 2013.

As they released these albums, they started to do more elaborate videos that went viral, with covers of songs of Daft Punk, Radioactive, Can't Hold Us, and many more. Their YouTube subscribers began to grow exponentially. They were getting millions of views for every video and their immense success of the third album, and they started gaining six thousand to seven thousand subscribers a day. It was too difficult to have Penta Parties.

In May 2014, Pentatonix left Madison Gate and signed with RCA Records, a "flagship" label of Sony Music Entertainment. What caught the attention of RCA Records was "Little Drummer Boy," which peaked at number thirteen on the *Billboard* Hot 100, in December 2013, which they *almost* didn't post. Scott said, "Tom Corson at RCA got pushback on signing us, but he insisted he saw potential."

Fortunately, after the "Epic" failure, they secured an exceptional legal team that consistently prioritized their best interests, including artistic freedom and fair compensation. In fact, when RCA sought to sign them, Pentatonix lawyers negotiated a deal so favorable that even they were astounded by its terms.

The same year they signed with RCA, their fourth EP, *PTX, Vol. III* was released, charting number five on the *Billboard* 200. They didn't stop there though. They released two full-length studio albums, *PTX, Vols. 1 & 2*, and a compilation album for Japan, Korea, and Australia. After that, they released their second holiday album, *That's Christmas to Me*, on October 21, 2014, a pivotal point in their upward climb, particularly in the holiday genre. The album was certified Gold (five hundred thousand copies sold) on December 10, 2014. Just two weeks later, on December 24, it was certified Platinum (one million copies sold). It reached Double Platinum status (two million copies sold) on February 11, 2016, and peaked at number two on the *Billboard* 200, only being topped by Taylor Swift's *1989*. *That's Christmas to Me* made history as the highest-charting holiday album by a group since 1962. Additionally, it claimed the position of the fourth-best-selling album in the United States in 2014.

In 2015, Pentatonix released their self-titled album consisting mostly of original material, which debuted at number one on the US *Billboard* 200 for the first time in their career. Their third Christmas album, *A Pentatonix Christmas*, also reached number one on the *Billboard* 200. In 2016, a new EP, *PTX IV Classics*, debuted at number four on the US *Billboard* 200 chart. In total, they have done seven Christmas albums/EPs and seven non-Christmas albums/EPs.

Out of all these albums, Pentatonix has been nominated for a Grammy five times and has won three: They were the first a cappella act to win Best Arrangement Instrumental or A Cappella, for "Daft Punk" in 2015 and "Dance of the Sugarplum Fairies" in 2016, and Best Country Duo/Group Performance in 2017 for "Jolene," a collaboration with Dolly Parton. The other two nominations came in 2022 and 2023, both for Best Traditional Pop Vocal Album. In 2022, the group received a star on the Hollywood Walk of Fame. As of July 2024, Pentatonix has over twenty million subscribers on their YouTube channel and 6 billion views. The group's video version of "Hallelujah" alone has over 748 million views.

There is no question that PTX has solidified their status as a powerhouse in a cappella—a genre that matters, even if Epic didn't see that—and the music industry as a whole. Several years after Epic dropped them, an RCA executive showed Scott an email he received from an Epic exec, "We made a huge mistake regarding PTX." No kidding!

It is a credit to the group that they didn't let the supposed experts determine their course or change them. They stayed true to what they loved and believed in creatively, and they taught the music industry a lesson in the process.

In the fall of 2012, Pentatonix embarked on their first national headlining tour. It was sold out and spanned thirty cities. Whenever they were in Dallas for concerts or promotional events, Kevin Olusola and Avi Kaplan, accompanied by their first tour manager, Ben Bram, who later would be replaced by their permanent tour manager, Esther Kaplan Koop, found a home away from home at our house. Kirstie and Mitch would come over for practices and meetings. Listening to the group's harmonies at the house was mesmerizing, and I was amazed at the sounds they could create. On one of these visits, I came home from work and heard what I thought was an entire drum set being played. I asked Rick if he went out and got a drum set. He laughed and told me, "Nope, that's Kevin."

The group had a strong connection with their fans during those early tours. They had—and still have—a dedicated fan base, which calls itself "Pentaholics" and continues to support Pentatonix. During those early tours, PTX all packed in a twelve-seater van and would sleep on the drives. Scott told me recently, "I'm glad we had the rough and tough tour experience because now we can truly appreciate having the luxuries of a tour bus." The venues were relatively small, so there was much more time and space to talk with and get to know their supporters. However, the goal was clear—they wanted to sell out these smaller spaces and go bigger. It was a time when the group, although getting more popular, stayed connected to the core values of genuine connection and gratitude.

In addition to hosting Kevin, Avi, and Ben while they were in town, Rick and I became "roadies" and manned the merchandise table, chatting with fans and sharing our enthusiasm for the music. It was an incredible experience, feeling the sense of community across generations and being a part of it. When you go to a Pentatonix concert, it's not unusual to see an entire family with multiple generations—a young child, teenager, mom, and grandmother—all energized and excited about the show.

Despite the smaller venues, the vibe at PTX concerts was electrifying. They started regularly selling out these smaller venues, and more performance opportunities emerged. Thanks to *Glee*, *Pitch Perfect*, and *The Sing-Off*, there was a growing interest in a cappella music and PTX's unique spin on it. Fans were also drawn to their authenticity and passion, venues kept getting bigger, and tours kept getting longer. Audiences have always been impressed by how closely their live performances match the quality of their studio-recorded music.

These early memories of PTX coming to town, staying at our house, and watching them work are warm memories for me. There is something to be said for those small, more intimate shows, but when I walk into a sold-out ten-thousand to fifteen-thousand-seat venue, the pride and emotion is something else—indescribable.

———

And they would get there thanks to their musical talents, commitment, and the wonderful team behind them, most of whom have been with PTX almost since the beginning of their journey. Many of them have also contributed to Scott's solo projects, which include solo EPs, Superfruit, Citizen Queen, Acapop Kids, and even musicals.

Ken Phillips (publicist). Ken was PTX's publicist during their early years, playing a crucial role in moving their careers forward. His efforts in promoting the group helped them gain the visibility and recognition needed to reach a wider audience and establish their presence in the music industry. Ken's expertise and dedication were instrumental in shaping the public image of Pentatonix, setting the stage for their subsequent success.

Over the years, Ken and I have kept in touch, maintaining a close friendship. I am forever grateful to him for introducing me to my current publisher for this book. His support and connections have been important in both the early success of Pentatonix and my personal journey in writing a book.

Ben Bram (arranger). An alumnus of USC, he played a significant role in persuading Scott to try out for *The Sing-Off*. After PTX won *The Sing-Off*, Ben assumed the role of their tour manager and helped with arrangements of their songs. His collaborative effort with Pentatonix on "Daft Punk" earned him a Grammy in 2015. He is a gifted young man, and I am so grateful that he came into Scott's life in 2010.

Jake Updegraff (social media). Scott and Jake met through a mutual friend in 2012. They became good friends, and Scott hired him to help with socials for Scott and Mitch's side project, Superfruit. Scott was so impressed with the social engagement that he suggested the band hire Jake. Management reached out, and he took the job.

His first job was touring North America and Europe for their *On My Way Home* tour in 2015. He did all the social media platforms for them and, more than a decade later, he's still doing it. Jake's independent business has grown significantly, and he has several superstar clients including Kelly Clarkson, David Archuleta, Alicia Silverstone, and Ally Brooke from Fifth Harmony, to name a few. He is not only one of the most talented social media gurus, but he is one of the nicest people you will ever meet.

Candice McAndrews (stylist). Candice has been the stylist for PTX, Superfruit, and all of Scott's solo projects. Her impressive portfolio also includes styling for Kelly Clarkson, Bon Jovi, the Eagles, the Doobie Brothers, and many others. If you've ever wondered why PTX always look so amazing, Candice is the reason. Candice has been with PTX since 2014, when the creative director at RCA called and asked her to style the group. When RCA calls for styling advice, you know that person has some serious talent, and she absolutely does. She told me her goal was to make them a cohesive unit while still allowing each member to maintain their own identity, a balance she achieves effortlessly.

Thomas McAndrews (manager for solo projects). Thomas, Candice's husband, is Scott's manager for all his solo projects, playing a crucial role in shaping Scott's solo career. Interestingly, Tom used to be Bon Jovi's manager, which is how he and

Candice met. Scott is incredibly fortunate to have both Candice and Tom in his life, not just as a stylist and manager, but as friends and mentors.

Lindsey Blaufarb (with Craig Hollamon) (choreographer). Lindsey is an amazing choreographer and over the years has become one of Scott's best friends. When PTX recorded their first original album, they needed a choreographer for the video "Can't Sleep Love." Lindsey had just finished a tour for Avril Lavigne and came highly recommended by Gee One (a member of Jabbawockeez). Scott absolutely adores her, and the chemistry between them is amazing. She does more than choreo, too, as they will get together and plan sets, lights, and props. She and her assistant, Craig Hollamon, find specific dancers for whatever they need. She has not just worked on PTX videos and tours but has done all the videos requiring choreo for Superfruit and Scott's solo projects, as well as for Acapop Kids and Citizen Queen. She is titled creative director for Scott's solo projects, though she humbly states it is more like a cocreative director position with Scott.

Lindsey has gone above and beyond by helping me learn dance routines for TikToks (one that went superviral) and choreographed a hip-hop song for Rick and me to perform at Scott's wedding. Her extensive résumé speaks volumes about her talent and experience. Lindsey's work has graced numerous concerts, YouTube videos, and even movies, showcasing her versatility and creativity as a choreographer. Lindsey's impact on Scott's life is significant, and I know Scott is incredibly grateful to have her guiding him through each step, both literally and figuratively.

Sara Baczewski (manager), Alexis Lowes, Sarah Crossland (tour management team). These three are the cream of the crop when it comes to management skills. Sara B., the head manager, is the backbone of the band's business operations. She handles everything from bookings, scheduling, promotion, and so much more, allowing PTX to focus on their creative work while ensuring that all aspects of their career are managed effectively. Alexis, the tour manager, and Sarah, the tour assistant, make up the tour management team and play a crucial role in the success of concert tours, including world tours. They coordinate travel, manage tour expenses and schedules, address any issues that come up during the tour, and do a hundred other things that are necessary for a band to function smoothly. I have been to many concerts and events worldwide (thanks to this team), and everything always runs seamlessly. PTX are so fortunate to have them on their team.

Mario Jose (former tour assistant). During an interview, Mario mentioned that he and Scott had crossed paths a few times at *The Sing-Off* tapings, but they officially met at the Spaulding Sessions, a house concert Ben Bram hosted in early 2012. Pentatonix performed, and afterward, Mario sang.

It was then that Scott approached him, asking, "Umm, why didn't you tell me you *sang* like that?!" That was the start of their over a decade-long friendship. As their friendship grew, Mario would go to all of their shows that he could and help sell merchandise, usually alongside Ryan Parma and other friends. Then he did a short West Coast tour with them in 2013, selling merch and assisting wherever possible.

In 2015, Scott officially invited Mario to be their tour assistant on the North American leg of the *On My Way Home* tour. He has performed with Pentatonix many times on their tours, sang background vocals on two Pentatonix albums, *PTXmas* and *A Pentatonix Christmas*, and recorded several YouTube covers with Scott and Superfruit. Mario told me that he, Scott, and Ben Bram cowrote the title track of his debut EP *Heart Of Gold*, which debuted at number thirty-three on the iTunes Pop Charts! While he is now focused on his solo career, he was indispensable during PTX's early years, readily assisting with anything they needed. His positive demeanor and helpful nature made him a valuable presence within the group.

Ryan Parma (director/videographer). Ryan met Scott at Ben Bram's house when he was asked to video some singers that night at the Spaulding Sessions. One of them was Pentatonix. He did a great job and was hired to do some videos for Pentatonix. Some of the first ones were "Ah Ha," "We Are Young," "Disney's Teen Beach Music Medley," the first PTXperience, and many more over the years. He is a talented videographer/director and has done multiple videos for PTX, Superfruit, and Scott's solo projects, including "Acapop Kids" and "Citizen Queen." Ryan is one of the most talented videographers and nicest people you will ever meet.

Genevieve Lamb (hair and makeup artist). Another gem RCA connected PTX with was Genevieve Lamb. Scott met Genevieve when she was invited to tour with PTX as their dedicated hair and makeup artist for their 2015 *On My Way Home* documentary. Despite initial nerves about leaving in just four days and being away for five weeks without knowing anyone on the tour, she embraced the opportunity.

It turned out to be an amazing experience, leading to several more tours with PTX around the world. Although she had to quit touring when she started having children, she remains close to the band, handling their hair and makeup for local events. We bonded during the Europe and Japan tours, and she has done my makeup for all five of the Grammy shows. Genevieve and Scott share a strong friendship, and we often see her at various events or during her visits when we're at Scott's house. She is a beautiful person, inside and out, and I am grateful to have met her through PTX.

Joey Orton, Brad Silnutzer, and Petro AP (musical collaborators). Scott met these geniuses when he attended their musical, *Fast and Furious.* After the show they talked for quite a while backstage and hit it off instantly. When Scott was getting ready to leave, he stated, "If you ever want to collaborate on some things, let me know." Well, that's all it took, and soon they were creating

TikToks and then a full-blown musical that is set to premiere in New York City in 2025.

———

It truly takes a team to make it in music. Scott had us when he was young, and then he gained all of these talented individuals, many of whom have become a chosen second family. And this chosen family has skills—more, if you can believe it, than I had dancing in those TikTok videos.

Chapter 11

Superfruit

Scott also had some important side projects throughout these years. About a year after Pentatonix got started, Scott and Mitch decided to start a YouTube channel. I'll never forget the story Scott shared with me about the start of Superfruit. Over pancakes at IHOP amid casual chatter about their individual aspirations for YouTube channels, Scott casually proposed the idea of collaborating. "Maybe we could do one together," he suggested.

Mitch's immediate enthusiasm sealed the deal as he exclaimed, "Yes, let's call it Superfruit."

And just like that, over a breakfast table, Superfruit was born. Many people don't know that they originally planned to be an anonymous rap duo and release intense rap music and not tell anyone who they were, but they decided against it.

First thing, Scott had to learn a new skill set. Ryan Parma, his good friend, videographer, and director, taught him how to edit, produce, outline episodes, set up DSLR cameras, film, and lighting skills. Scott would then upload and promote hundreds of videos for Superfruit. Scott has said, "It was an insane amount of work, but it taught me so many skills."

Initially, the set was pretty simple, like the background look of PTX videos—just a couch with a picture behind them. Then they added lights and a better camera. The content included funny banter, weekly obsessions, skits, games, guests, and lots of music. On August 13, 2013, Scott called and told me Superfruit was being launched that day. He was so excited for me to watch it, and he wanted me to let him know what I thought. I believed it was brilliant and that it would do so well. It gained a following quickly due to their chemistry, wit, vocals, and unique content, taking them to places that none of us expected (well, I expected it).

I've enjoyed many of their videos for different reasons. In their hilarious "Frozen Melody" parody, they invited Kirstie to join in, and it was pure comedy gold. From using Kirstie's hair as wigs to their incredible vocals and playful acting, the entire performance was a riot. The best part was watching them try to keep a straight face, which only made it funnier for everyone else. Another standout is their rendition of "Defying Gravity" for the stunning and emotional vocals that make it an unforgettable performance. Other personal favorites include two mashups of hip-hop songs going Broadway with clever arrangements and amazing vocals. The bloopers at the end of each are hilarious, making them even more enjoyable.

By 2016, they had grown to over two million subscribers on YouTube, so they decided to use that to start promoting music. They released their first original song, "Bad4 Us," on October 18 and "Sweet Life" on November 15. Under the RCA label, they released 2 EPs, *Future Friends Part One* on June 30, 2017, and *Part Two* on September 15, 2017. It charted at twenty-nine in the United States. While releasing songs, they were also posting videos on YouTube for each song on the two EPs.

One day, I told Scott that my favorite song was "Guy.exe." He laughed and said he had written that song in fifteen minutes. I must have been right, though, since it has over two hundred million streams and was a major TikTok trend worldwide. It even had multiple resurgences on TikTok as a trending sound for a bit in 2023. It was certified Gold by the Recording Industry Association of America in August 2024 for selling 500,000 units.

Superfruit's music was different from Pentatonix since it featured electronic instruments. There was no Christmas music. They began to tour, selling out venues and having television interviews and performances. In 2017, they received, along with their choreographers, Lindsey B. and Craig, a World Choreography Award for "Best Choreography in a Music Video" for the single "Sweet Life."

They were featured on Betty Who's "Beautiful" from her album *The Valley*, and they were a featured artist on *Kesha's Weird and Wonderful Rainbow Cruise* in February 2019. They did an MTV commercial promoting *The Spongebob Movie: Sponge Out of Water*, and Mitch got a SpongeBob tattoo for the commercial. They had also received an offer to have their own TV show, which they developed for six months, but it didn't work out. Superfruit

Figure 11.1   Scott and Mitch. Luke Fontana.

attained 2.41 million subscribers and had 481.2 million views on YouTube prior to them stepping away from the project.

I've had many Superfruit fans ask me why they stopped. Scott has basically said that their friendship was more important, that the show took an insane amount of work, filming, and pressure to keep up the silly, high-energy vibes. As they got older, it started to take a toll on them, and they started to want different things. They stepped away to have more personal creative freedom and to not implode their friendship.

All of their videos are still on YouTube if you want to see some funny and entertaining shows. It was fun while it lasted—a different energy and sound.

CHAPTER 12

International Success
and the Grammys

Pentatonix has been our family's passport to the whole world, taking us to several countries in Europe, Singapore, Japan, and elsewhere—places that I never dreamed of visiting. Scott, Rick, and I have often talked about our favorite places and the venues we love most for PTX concerts. There were a few places where we were all in agreement that were the best and had such special memories.

The Hollywood Bowl remains one of Scott's all-time favorite venues. Pentatonix has performed there on three occasions, each more memorable than the last. In 2013, they opened for Diana Ross. It was a surreal experience for Scott and the group, as they were just starting out fresh off their win on *The Sing-Off*. The second time was over the Fourth of July in 2017, when they performed three consecutive sold-out nights. Scott said it was an incredibly special experience because the atmosphere was electric, and his family and his LA friends were all there to share it with him. We went to all three shows that holiday weekend and all of them were fantastic.

The 2022 Hollywood Bowl show was Scott's favorite show of all time. The energy in the audience was off the charts, and the USC SoCal VoCals joined them to provide background vocals

Figure 12.1 Hollywood Bowl. Author's family photo.

for "Bohemian Rhapsody." We were there, too, and it's a night we'll never forget. ♪

Madison Square Garden is another of Scott's favorite venues, as well as ours. Pentatonix has performed there several times, and each show has been a thrilling experience. Scott has always said, "Singing at the iconic Madison Square Garden feels like the epitome of success." He remembers being at a Wingstop with a friend in 2017 and telling him that one of his goals was to sing at Madison Square Garden. I completely agree with Scott—it is truly iconic.

On one visit to this venue, Rick and I had some free time and decided to wander around on our own. At one point, we got lost and took a wrong turn. We ended up going through some double doors and, to our surprise, we walked into a room filled with what seemed like fifty seven-foot-tall men. We had accidentally stumbled into a room of the entire New York Knicks' team while they were eating. It was pretty awkward when they all turned to look at us. No free lunch here, but such great memories!

Pentatonix has also performed outside of the United States, and the time in Europe, we all agree, was truly amazing. In

Figure 12.2 Pentatonix performs at Madison Square Garden! Author's family photo.

2015, Pentatonix set out on their first European tour to reach and engage with their international fanbase, and they performed in several major cities. Most of our family joined them in Paris, Cologne, Amsterdam, and Antwerp. Lindsay was deployed and unable to join us.

We couldn't wait to start exploring Paris, but we had a rough start once we arrived. After an easy taxi ride from the airport to our hotel, there was an unexpected challenge. Scott wanted to meet at the Eiffel Tower, and we were excited to join him. Rick, Lauren, Robbie (Lauren's husband), and I walked across the street to take the Paris Metro to the tower. Rick bought the tickets, and as we were heading to the train, he noticed his wallet was missing. We hurried back to the ticket office, hoping he had left it there, but the agent said it wasn't there. We couldn't believe it—Rick's wallet had been stolen within an hour of arriving in France.

We rushed back to the hotel to cancel all our credit cards. Fortunately, I had one card that Rick didn't have, so we used that for the entire trip. Rick also had all the euros that we had just exchanged at the airport in his wallet. It was a nightmare, but we managed to work it out and not let it get us down. This incident was a definite lesson learned, and since that trip, Rick has kept his wallet in a safe spot. No, I won't tell you where!

We finally made it to the subway station near the Champ de Mars. The Eiffel Tower came into view, towering against the sky with its iron structure even more impressive up close. We met up with Scott and took the elevator to the top. The view was stunning, and we saw the Notre Dame Cathedral, the Louvre, and the Seine River from one thousand feet up. After we came down, we went to a nearby café and enjoyed croissants and French wine. The following evening, we went to the PTX concert at the Bataclan, a perfect end to our Parisian adventure.

———

Another highlight of our European trip was the city of Amsterdam. We were anxious to see the city known for its canals, culture, and fantastic architecture. After checking into our hotel, the Atlas Vondelpark, we freshened up and set out to explore. We walked along the cobblestone streets and marveled at the seventeenth-century houses lining the waterways. There were bicycles everywhere, rushing by us, to places unknown. We even visited the famous Anne Frank House, which was a deeply moving experience. Reading through her personal writings of the unimaginable hardships she and her family endured was heart wrenching.

The next day, we toured Keukenhof Gardens, one of the world's most extensive flower gardens. Keukenhof has millions of tulips, daffodils, hyacinths, and other stunning flowers. We spent hours walking around the grounds until it was time to go back and get ready for the PTX concert. That evening, we went to the iconic Paradiso to watch Pentatonix perform. As we approached the building, we saw a line of people that seemed like a mile long. We enjoyed an amazing concert and went out afterward with Scott to have our last visit with him since we were heading home the next day. Without a doubt, Amsterdam was my favorite place in Europe.

In September 2016, during PTX's world tour, Rick, Lauren, and I were fortunate enough to join Scott and PTX in Singapore. Scott's twenty-fifth birthday coincided with the trip, so it was a special occasion. His birthday celebration took place on the roof-top of a building called Guaca Tower, which looked out over the beautiful city of Singapore.

We started the evening with hors d'oeuvres and champagne, which were presented to Scott with sparklers coming out of them, followed by a delicious cake. Afterward, we moved downstairs to the indoor club and continued the celebration. The club featured a light show with the message "Happy Birthday, Scott" that kept circling on the walls. Everyone danced and had a great time. I'm sure it's a birthday Scott will never forget—I know I won't!

PTX had several performances in Singapore, including their performance at the Formula One Grand Prix race. They performed before the race, and then we were escorted to the luxurious suite reserved for PTX and crew: great food and drinks, an incredible vantage point to watch the race, and plenty of space to relax and socialize. When the race finished, we had a convoy of police officers on motorcycles escort us back to the hotel, which was surreal.

Scott and I agree that Japan is one of our favorite places in the world. In the spring of 2017, I went on an extraordinary trip to Japan to meet up with Scott and Pentatonix. They were on a nine-city tour, and Scott invited me to go along. (He invited his dad, too, but Rick had to work.) The seventeen-hour flight felt like an eternity, but I was so excited to get there that fatigue was not an issue. The incredible adventure began as the plane touched down at Narita International Airport in Tokyo.

Esther, the amazing tour manager, had taken care of every detail. She made sure I had a driver to get me from the airport to the hotel where PTX was staying. She booked all my hotel rooms, arranged my train rides from city to city, and made reservations for all the excursions. I was included in all the restaurant reservations as well. It was my first time trying sake, and it was unlike anything I had ever tasted before. Each time we moved to a new city, my bags would be picked up, and magically, I'd find them in the next hotel room. I had never experienced anything like that in my life, and it was amazing.

The tour kicked off in Tokyo, the capital city. Tokyo was both modern and traditional and stunningly beautiful. Pentatonix had their first show at the famous Nippon Budokan, and the house was packed. As we arrived at the venue, it seemed like thousands of fans were waiting to go inside. Word had spread that I was traveling with the group, and soon enough, fans were swarming me, asking for selfies. This happened at every concert, and I felt like a star—it was so much fun! By the fourth concert, I was hanging out in Scott's dressing room as showtime approached. Scott turned to me and said, "Mom, you should probably go meet your fans."

By this point in the tour, I was pretty exhausted, so I told him, "I'll go out later tonight, I'm really tired."

He jokingly responded, "Mom, you've only been doing this a few days, and you're over it already,"

Everyone in the room laughed at our exchange, and Scott still tells this story to this day.

Other cities we enjoyed included Nagoya, where we saw the Nagoya Castle during Scott's break. Other concerts were in Osaka, Hiroshima, and several other cities, eventually ending up in Yokohama, just a short distance from Tokyo. The last show was in a huge stadium and was a full house. My fans awaited, and I did not disappoint (haha).

The 2017 Japan tour was an incredible journey. Each city offered its own unique experiences, and the warm reception from fans made the tour truly special, especially for me.

———

We've been fortunate enough to attend some of PTX's performances at big sporting events, like the Kentucky Derby and World Series playoffs. But the most memorable one for us was when they sang the national anthem at the NCAA College Football Championship game in January 2023. Thanks to PTX's tour manager, Alexis Lowes, she managed to secure last-minute tickets for Rick and me.

After a travel delay, we arrived at SoFi Stadium, just in the nick of time. It was extra special because our hometown college, TCU, was playing, and our next-door neighbor was a backup quarterback.

Rick and I were in the suite almost by ourselves while PTX was on the field getting ready to sing. Their rendition of the anthem was nothing short of spectacular, and it is still my favorite. Afterward, they joined us, and we enjoyed unlimited food and drinks as we mingled with everyone. Unfortunately, our TCU Horned Frogs were unsuccessful. We thought, *There's always next year!*

Figure 12.3 PTX performs the national anthem at the college football championships. Author's family photo.

The Kentucky Derby was also memorable when PTX performed there in 2018. Esther secured tickets to the Derby for Rick and me, along with passes to the Pentatonix suite. Unable to get a hotel room, we pulled our teardrop trailer to a campsite about a mile from Churchill Downs. The drive was a challenge since a massive thunderstorm was right behind us. The radar looked like a scene from a disaster movie, so we were practically flying to stay ahead of it.

When we finally arrived, we found our site and set up the trailer. It was pretty quiet, with no one on either side of us. We decided to make a quick grocery run before the storm hit. An hour later, we returned to find two behemoth RVs, the size of tour buses, parked on either side of our tiny trailer. It was like a mouse squeezed between two elephants.

As we were putting things away, we met our new neighbors: on one side, a group of girls on a bachelorette weekend and, on the other, a bunch of guys on a bachelor weekend. What are the odds? Initially, I braced myself for a noisy, sleepless weekend, and while it was loud and crazy, they were a fantastic bunch who invited us to join the fun. Of course, we couldn't resist.

Scott and Esther came by to drop off our tickets and passes. Scott had never seen our little trailer, and to see it between those two RV giants must have been such a sight. Both of them could barely stifle their laughter. That evening, we had a blast with our new friends, barbecuing, playing games, and swapping stories. And we actually got some sleep too.

At the track the next day, everyone was so dressed up with large hats, myself included. We walked to Churchill Downs and found our suite. No one was there yet because PTX had taken a red-eye flight and had an eight o'clock sound check. They went back to their hotel and slept for a while. Meanwhile, Rick and I indulged in the delicious food and mint juleps and placed bets on the early races. Our suite was near the finish line, offering a perfect view of the action.

Gradually, PTX members and crew started arriving. Everyone looked amazing, and we all made bets. However, I did feel bad for our camp neighbors. The pouring rain had begun, and I knew they were outdoors in the infield. They had to be soaked, and if I remember correctly, you weren't allowed to have umbrellas, only ponchos.

I still can't believe we were able to attend such an incredible event, and I still keep in touch with some of our camp neighbors on Facebook. Pentatonix and their management have been amazing to us, and we can't express our gratitude enough, despite the poor showing of my favorite horse that day.

———

I have been so fortunate to attend five Grammys and could write a story about each of them. However, I will just recount the most recent one as of this writing, February 2024. Pentatonix had earned their fifth Grammy nomination for their album *Holidays around the World*. Lindsay and I attended this event, and it did not disappoint. We attended pre-Grammy parties, gifting suites, the actual Grammys, and after parties.

Between Grammy festivities, Scott gave us performances of his latest original songs and snippets from his musical projects while sharing about his other endeavors. It was absolutely mind-blowing.

On the day of the Grammys, Lindsay and I spent several hours with makeup artist Genevieve Lamb and hairstylist Kelly Wood. It was Genevieve's fifth time doing my makeup. They are so talented, and we had a lot of fun with them while getting beautified.

When we left the house, the sky was clear, but it was sprinkling by the time we got to the Crypto Center. We got dropped off close to the venue, so there was no threat to Kelly and Genevieve's hard work yet. We went in for the streamed but nontelevised part of the Grammys. Pentatonix was doing the opening number with Jordin Sparks, Larkin Poe, J. Ivy, and Sheila E. before the awards were announced. I remember when I started going to the Grammys, I had no idea that there were so many Grammy awards given that aren't actually televised. Kind of a shame, really, there were so many talented performers.

We had a couple of hours before the televised part of the Grammys, so we decided to get lunch. We walked to the door, and to our surprise, it was raining so hard you could hardly see.

The restaurant was about one hundred yards away. We couldn't find umbrellas to purchase, so we bought ball caps. We sprinted to the restaurant as best we could in heels. We were soaked, but Lindsay has a way of making me laugh in these kinds of moments. Besides, isn't the wet look in now?

We stayed at the restaurant for about two hours, waiting for the rain to stop. That didn't happen, so we had to walk to the Crypto Center, getting wetter by the minute. We put our ball caps back on and took off for our designated Crypto Center entrance. We couldn't run because thousands of people were walking in the same direction. Everyone had umbrellas, and I said to Lindsay, "I guess we missed the 'bring an umbrella' memo." Halfway there, an English gentleman asked me if I wanted to share his umbrella. Even though I was already soaked, I agreed, and he walked me to the front door. Thank you, whoever you were!

We saw performances by Billie Eilish, Olivia Rodrigo, Billy Joel, Brandi Carlile, and Joni Mitchell during the event. Amazing!

We could see Scott and the group sitting closer to the stage. They were seated next to an opera singer Scott said was a Pentatonix fan; Scott said she was very sweet. He was also near Oprah Winfrey, who was talking with Miley Cyrus—so much star power.

After the Grammys, we walked to the hotel, and it was still raining. My shoes were soaked and hard to walk in, so I left the glamorous Grammys with my shoes in my hand, walking back to the hotel with bare feet. PTX arrived shortly after us to get ready for the Sony after-party. Scott told us back at the hotel room that the highlight of the night for him was when Taylor Swift announced the upcoming release of her album *The Tortured Poets Department* right after winning a Grammy. He was also excited that he ran into the SoCal Vocal music director from when he attended USC.

Figure 12.4 Lindsay and Connie getting soaked on the way to the Grammys. Author's family photo.

We all rode together to the Sony party, and while there, I ended up not even twenty feet from Billy Joel. I wish I had the courage to go over and talk to him. We stayed a few hours and returned to the hotel, looking pretty much like drowned water rats. It didn't matter. Wet or not, I had been twenty feet from Billy Joel!

———

Scott also has a soft spot for the Kennedy Center in Washington DC, where he's performed a couple of times. In 2014, Pentatonix was invited to perform at the Kennedy Center Honors, an annual ceremony that celebrates those in the performing arts for their lifetime contributions to American culture. That year, Tom Hanks was one of the honorees. Pentatonix sang "That Thing You Do!"—a song from the movie by the same name that Tom Hanks directed and starred in. After the ceremony, Hanks typed a heartfelt letter to each member of Pentatonix using an actual "old time" typewriter. Scott was especially touched by this and had the letter framed. It still hangs in his house today.

Pentatonix was asked back to the Kennedy Center in May 2021. That year, legendary Dick Van Dyke was among the honorees, an icon whom I grew up loving and watching on TV and movies. Pentatonix performed "Chitty Chitty Bang Bang" from the movie of the same name as a tribute to him. Scott was particularly thrilled about this performance because he had always been inspired by Dick Van Dyke—from all the way back when he performed "Put on a Happy Face" in elementary school. He has also long dreamed of portraying him in a biographical movie. After having a few drinks, Scott got the courage to approach Van Dyke at an after-party, hoping to tell him how much he admired him and share his movie idea. He even did a few of Van Dyke's iconic dance steps. "I bet you'd be perfect for the role," Van Dyke responded.

After talking for a while, Scott offered to get him a drink. Van Dyke politely declined, saying that he hadn't consumed alcohol in almost fifty years. Scott asked him what life was like postdrinking, and he said that it was one of the best decisions he ever made. Scott was inspired that night and decided to quit drinking for three months. During those months, he lost twenty pounds. Scott felt so good that he decided to go for six months. By the end of six months, he had lost another ten pounds and felt a surge in his energy and creativity. It was then that he decided to make the change permanent.

Scott has not had a drink since that night in May 2021 and now makes the same claim as Dick Van Dyke: it was the best decision he ever made. Scott believes maybe the universe was telling him, "It's time to chill out on the drinking." It was extra special that the universe delivered that message in the form of a singing and dancing legend!

Scott's life with PTX has brought him so many thrilling experiences—from travel to awards ceremonies and, along the way, he has met icons in the industry. We have been able to travel along at times, Scott's success coloring our world. We may not have been inspired to make any life changes the way Scott was that evening with Dick Van Dyke, but we have all changed for the better.

Boy Meets Boy

Sometimes the universe knows when you are ready for love.

Scott came out publicly through a video, Pentatonix's rendition of John Lennon's "Imagine" in 2017. Right after the group shot that video, Scott met Mark Manio at a mutual friend's birthday party. Instantly smitten with each other, Scott couldn't wait to share all the details with me over the phone. His excitement was obvious, gushing about Mark for nearly an hour. Hearing his enthusiasm, I couldn't help but think, "This might just be the one." Scott later told me that he felt that coming out, with its newfound freedom, allowed him to finally and truly fall in love.

In the past, I often heard Scott wonder if he would ever find true love. Now that he has, I couldn't be happier. My hope and dream for all three of my children was for them to find a relationship like the one Rick and I have cherished for over four decades. Rick and I are truly soulmates, and our children have seen that bond firsthand.

When Scott and Mark first started dating, Mark employed at Amazon Studios as a marketing specialist. A year later, he transitioned into freelance modeling and began landing jobs. He also works on numerous projects with Scott.

We first met Mark and spent time with him from July 2 to 4, 2017, when Pentatonix performed three consecutive evenings

Figure 13.1 Scott and Mark embrace during a photo shoot following their engagement. Lindsay Hoying Fondren.

at the Hollywood Bowl. This was Mark's first Pentatonix concert. Even though Mark planned for a vacation at this time, he changed his plans and flights in order to attend. We were at all three shows and spent a lot of time with Mark. We enjoyed dinners together, got to know Mark better, and wrapped up the third day with a fun Fourth of July party at Scott's house after the final performance. A few weeks after I met Mark, he sent me flowers for my birthday. It was so sweet and thoughtful, and it only solidified my admiration for him.

One month later, in August, we had another meeting with Mark in Tampa, Florida. Rick's siblings live in Florida, so he met nearly the entire Hoying family. From that point on, we started seeing Mark regularly at PTX concerts, and our bond with him grew quickly. Evidently, Scott and Mark's bond grew rapidly, too, and they started living together in April 2018; about one year after meeting.

It didn't take long for our entire family to think the world of Mark and for my grandchildren to start calling him "Uncle Mark." His authenticity and kindness won us over completely.

———

Mark has an innate creativity and is full of ideas. He started collaborating with Scott on songwriting, and their first song, "Thank You," is a personal favorite of mine, written during the pandemic to express gratitude for each other's support during the difficult lockdown period.

They coauthored a children's book during the lockdown, too, entitled "How Lucky Am I," which was released on May 21, 2024, and reached the *USA TODAY* bestseller list. It tells the story of a mayfly that lives for only twenty-four hours, emphasizing the importance of living each day to the fullest and cherishing the ones you love. They also cowrote a song for the book, which they performed together on the *Tamron Hall Show*, and as of this writing, they are working on a second children's book.

I love watching Scott and Mark bounce ideas off each other and then realize those ideas, creating amazing songs, books, TikToks, and videos. Their social media platforms showcase their creative process and ability to communicate as well as joyful moments between the two in heartfelt displays of love for each other.

Along with these projects, all initiated during the COVID-19 pandemic, Scott wrote hundreds of his songs. Out of these songs, he released a solo EP in July 2023 with seven of his favorites. Most of them were love letters to Mark, as he wanted to immortalize this exciting moment in life into art.

Additionally, Mark took charge of managing the group Citizen Queen. This group was started right before the pandemic. It immediately got a record deal with RCA and opened for Pentatonix on their Christmas tour of 2019. Their debut EP *CLIQUE* was released in 2023 and has gotten millions of streams on Spotify, millions of views on their music videos on YouTube, and millions of followers on TikTok and Instagram. The members—Nina, Cora, and Kaedi—are immensely talented, and I truly believe they deserve to be a household name.

After six years of being together Scott decided to pop the question during a trip to the Bahamas. The year was 2022, and Pentatonix was there for a show, which happened to coincide with Mark's birthday. Under the guise of a romantic beachside dinner to celebrate his birthday, Scott surprised Mark.

Scott dropped to one knee and asked for Mark's hand in marriage. There were laughter, tears . . . and a "*Yes!*"

It was an incredibly touching moment. Scott filmed it, and you can find the moment on his social media.

A few days after the proposal, Rick and I flew to the Bahamas to celebrate with them. Our entire family was so happy for them, and we couldn't wait to hug them, congratulate them, and celebrate their engagement. We took them to dinner and got to hear every detail of their beachside engagement.

The next day we walked around the Atlantis resort and got in a little pool time. We then went to PTX's rehearsal and afterward went to dinner with the band and the crew. Everyone was there to celebrate Scott and Mark, and my heart was so full I thought it would explode.

During dinner, I noticed Scott seemed distracted. I asked him, "What are you doing over there?!" He showed me he had

Figure 13.2 Scott proposes to Mark on the beach in the Bahamas. Author's family photo.

already gone down the planning rabbit hole on Instagram, already saving hundreds of pictures for inspiration and brainstorming what kind of wedding they would have.

On our last day there, we went to the PTX concert, which was outdoors and on an absolutely beautiful evening. Afterward, we went back to Atlantis, visited with Scott and Mark, and said our goodbyes.

A fun tidbit, Meghan Trainor saw the "proposal" video on social media and contacted Scott to congratulate him. During that phone call, Meghan revealed to Scott that she was writing songs for her new album. He asked her if he could listen to some of them, and she said she'd love his thoughts. Scott listened to them immediately and was amazed! Feeling inspired, he recorded some choir parts and sent some other ideas over. Meghan loved them and excitedly asked him if he could come over the next day. Since then, they have become quite the collaborators. (More on that later.)

———

It took more than a year for Scott and Mark to plan the wedding. After getting engaged, they immediately hired the services of a wedding planning company called Orange Blossom Special Events, which did not disappoint. Together, Scott and Mark explored various locations across California in search of the ideal spot for the wedding. It took them nine months to find the perfect venue. I was getting a little nervous. If they didn't hurry up, they might not have been able to get the date they wanted, and "Save the Dates" needed to go out. They ultimately settled on the breathtaking Ritz-Carlton Bacara in Santa Barbara, nestled along the coastline.

Scott and Mark found out their wedding date was 7/7/7 (2023). This was moments after Scott met a sweet young girl named Seven at the NCAA college championship game, where she signed the national anthem for deaf audience members alongside Pentatonix as they sang it. After the game, they had a flight at 7:00 p.m. at gate 77 on a Boeing 777. When Scott and Mark landed, they got in the car, and the radio was on 97.7. The song playing was "Get Lucky." What are the odds!?

Over the next seven months, the wedding planners, Scott, and Mark dedicated themselves to creating the most spectacular wedding possible. Scott would frequently call to update me as the plans evolved, and his excitement and enthusiasm were evident as he described each new development. Each detail they shared painted a picture more enchanting than the last. I knew it was going to be incredible, and I couldn't wait for the special day.

—•—

Finally, the wedding week arrived. Rick and I flew out a few days early to enjoy beautiful Santa Barbara over the Fourth of July. Fortunately, Rick's family did the same, and we spent some family time together. We enjoyed meals, fireworks, the Pier, and seeing the sights of this beautiful city.

We arrived at the venue in the midafternoon of July 6. We were greeted by Scott and Mark and exchanged heartfelt greetings and hugs, making that first moment together so special. Scott and Mark had already taken care of our room reservation, and upon entering, we were welcomed with a beautiful gift basket containing delicious snacks and a bottle of red wine. Stepping out onto the balcony, we had a picturesque view of where the outdoor wedding would take place, as preparations for the stunning event were already underway.

We unpacked our bags and started getting ready for the wedding rehearsal and the evening's events. Both families gathered at the wedding area to prepare for the nuptials for the following day, and we all learned every detail of what to do to make the wedding go smoothly. The children were so excited to be a part of this special occasion and had a *very* hard time being still. By the end of the rehearsal, we felt prepared—we felt connected. Our two families were coming together as one.

After the wedding rehearsal, we had dinner in a wine cellar decorated with red roses and candles, and a string quartet played in the background. It was a romantic sight to behold and a teaser of how mind-blowing the next few days would be. The food was delicious, and the ambiance was magical. Every detail was just perfect.

Soon after the rehearsal dinner, we made our way to the welcome party. We were transported in golf carts to a beautiful outdoor venue covered with even more stunning flowers and a piano at the center. Hundreds of guests had already gathered, enjoying drinks and hors d'oeuvres.

As we socialized, Scott and Mark took their seats at the piano. Scott sang "Parallel," an original composition, and then friends and family were invited to come up and sing while Scott accompanied them on the piano.

The gathering was one of the most intimate and incredible concerts I have ever been to. Truly, it could have been a ticketed event. The lineup featured extraordinary talent including performances by Betty Who, Loren Allred, Rozzi Crane, Kirstie, Scott's sister Lauren, Mark's cousin Marina, Citizen Queen, Mario, and so many other gifted individuals. When the singing came to an end, guests were encouraged to write messages for Scott and Mark on the piano with gold Sharpies. That piano currently sits in the living room of their home for their future kids to play.

The wedding was the next day. It was outdoors with the ocean in the background, and thousands of white roses decorated the space. The wedding party consisted of Scott and Mark's siblings along with their spouses and all of their nieces and nephews. Rick and I accompanied Scott down the aisle first, and then after the bridal party finished walking down, Mark's parents escorted him to the altar.

Scott's youngest niece, Naomi, was a flower girl. After just three steps, she glanced up at all the people looking at her and then ran away. When the ceremony was over and people started leaving, Naomi had a change of heart. She gathered the flower petals and tossed them while walking down the aisle with newfound resolve. Everyone started clapping and cheering, and she finished her walk smiling from ear to ear. Scott put together a small video from different phone recordings to show her redemption arc and posted it on TikTok. It's pretty adorable.

Figure 13.3 Scott and Mark's welcome party. Author's family photo.

Scott and Mark stood under a flower arch, and Christina Perri presided over the ceremony. She also sang the song "A Thousand Years" during the wedding procession, a song she had originally written for a *Twilight* movie.

Scott and Mark's favorite movie scene of all time was the wedding scene from *Crazy Rich Asians*, where Kina Grannis sang, "Can't Help Falling in Love." Scott and Kina had met while

Figure 13.4 Mom and Dad escort Scott down the aisle. Heather Kincaid

Figure 13.5 Christina Perri officiated the wedding. Heather Kincaid

working under the same management team, collaborating on various projects, and became close friends. When Scott asked Kina to sing the same song from the movie at their wedding, she agreed without hesitation. They had always known they wanted that song to be part of their wedding day, and now it was coming from Kina Grannis herself. She sang it just as beautifully as in the movie, and hearing her perform it during the ceremony was incredibly special.

The couple shared their personally crafted vows, which were funny, heartfelt, and just beautiful. I was hit with waves of emotion, thinking back to my seventeen-year-old son, not knowing if he'd ever find love, be able to be himself, or even be able to get married legally but now professing the most beautiful vows I've ever heard. I breathed in deep trying to hold on to every detail of the moment.

After the ceremony, the guests departed for a cocktail hour while the wedding party and the couple's families stayed behind to take some pictures. As we finished up, we joined everyone at happy hour as we all waited for the reception room to open. Scott and Mark were very particular that no one should sneak a peek until it was time.

The moment arrived and the doors finally opened, inviting everyone inside.

I was immediately struck by a breathtaking scene as I stepped inside. It was unlike any reception or ceremony I had ever encountered before. The ballroom was fully blacked out, with mirrored tables and mirrored chairs, twinkling with thousands of lights reflecting off of every surface. It resembled a starry night sky with white roses in every corner.

Positioned on one side was Scott and Mark's giant, elevated, table, perched above the dance floor, almost like a stage. Scott does love the stage! Across from them, the DJ stood ready. My brother, Bill, told me later that he couldn't resist the urge to step back outside just to enter the room and experience the stunning sight once more.

Dinner commenced promptly, followed by heartfelt speeches from various loved ones—Mark's parents, Jamie and Liza, Rick

Figure 13.6 Kina Grannis performs "Can't Help Falling in Love." Author's family photo.

Figure 13.7 The first thing everyone saw as they entered the reception. Author's family photo.

and myself, Lindsay and Lauren, and Mark's sister, Christine. Prior to our speech, Rick and I had diligently rehearsed a dance routine to a Lil Nas X track, choreographed by Lindsey B. We performed it on the way up to give our speech, which was fun but definitely quite a ways outside our comfort zone.

Rick became quite the comedian during the speech, telling Cost n' Mayor, a spectacular dance duo, to eat their hearts out and thanking Lindsey B. for teaching and working with us for sixteen hours, which was funny considering the dance was very short and simple.

When the speeches were completed, Scott and Mark took to the dance floor for their first dance, accompanied by the powerful voice of Loren Allred singing "Never Enough" from *The Greatest Showman*, just as she did in the movie. Listening to the song on repeat is one of Scott and Mark's first memories as a couple.

Following the first dance, it was time for the mother-son dances. Scott and I danced to "The Rose," performed by Scott's sister, Lauren. I managed to keep it together, though my heart was about to burst.

Figure 13.8 Loren Allred performs "Never Enough" for Scott and Mark's first dance. Heather Kincaid

Mark and his mom shared a tender moment on the dance floor, dancing to the timeless melody of "What a Wonderful World."

Then Scott stepped up to the stage, as the DJ directed Mark to take a seat in the center of the dance floor. Scott sang to Mark a song he had written specifically for him two years prior to the wedding, titled "Four," which was about their four-year journey together. Seeing Mark's reaction and Scott's passion filled my heart. The second verse was about ice skating with their future daughter, and it's one of my favorite songs Scott has ever written.

After Mark's chair was relocated to the edge of the dance floor, he settled back into his seat. Scott, alongside Cost n' Mayor, Betty Who, Lindsey B., Craig, and a cadre of other dancers, delivered a performance to a Blackpink medley (Mark's favorite group) that left all of us astonished. I can't really describe it, but it can still be seen on Scott's TikTok channel. Within two hours of the dance being posted online, it had already amassed fifty million views. ♪

Following that, Mark's giant, beautiful, Filipino family, totaling around one hundred members, took to the floor and executed a choreographed dance routine to Pentatonix's original track, "Sing." I have no idea how they all found time to learn this choreo! It was spectacular. As they finished, the dancing music kicked in, and the floor was full for the remainder of the night. Scott felt overjoyed in this moment, and it was obvious he'd found the perfect family to join with ours.

Every detail about this wedding was unique yet tasteful and classic, even down to the cake. The cake looked like it was blowing in the wind but had frozen in time. The rest of the evening was filled with music and dancing. Scott and Mark curated a three-hour playlist in an *exact* order, separated into genres and eras of the night. The DJ said, "I'll follow the vibes and play by ear," and they responded with, "No, no, play this exact playlist in order from song one to song seventy." They are very particular about their music.

While everyone danced, there were other activities to enjoy. There was a photo booth that made the picture taken look like a magazine cover with "The Hoyings" across the top, and right below that it said, "We decided on forever & forever starts for us tonight."

Figure 13.9 Scott surprises Mark with a dance to a Blackpink medley. Heather Kincaid

A small tattoo parlor was set up in the corner for anyone who wanted a tattoo. Scott and Mark got matching tattoos on their forearms—777, so their luck will continue!

And of course, there was even more singing. Loren Allred's manager asked my daughter, Lauren, if she would sing a duet with Loren on the song "Never Enough." She was so excited to perform with Loren.

Around 1:00 a.m., the party came to a close. Everyone gathered outside the reception room, awaiting Scott and Mark's departure. Suddenly, white fireworks burst from poles along their path, creating a memorable spectacle as Mr. and Mr. Hoying left the party to start their new life together.

———

A few months after the wedding, Scott was on Jennifer Hudson's show, and she said, "I heard you got married." Scott responded with a big smile, shook his head yes, and flashed his wedding ring. Scott confided in me that at that moment, he felt a rush of emotions. The audience cheered, celebrating his love with his husband. For Scott, this moment was more than just a public announcement of his marriage. This was a profound change in how LGBTQ+ love was celebrated, compared to when he was younger. He was able to feel relaxed while publicly professing his love—no hesitation or small fear at the back of his mind. We are so fortunate to live in a time and place where he can be true to himself and embrace love openly and without shame.

Scott also thought about what it would have meant to him to see someone on television openly gay and supported when he was younger. He's grateful that he can be that for someone young and afraid to be themselves. There is hope, and things do get better. I have seen young gay men stop Scott on the street and talk about what he means to them. Those moments give me a powerful sense of hope for the future of our young people.

Chapter 14

Wedding Vows

Scott's vows to Mark:

Marky, I am so in awe of you. I want to cry every time I think about it . . . and I do! You are so unbelievably, mind-blowingly special, and I could feel it the moment I first met you at a random birthday party in West Hollywood that I spontaneously stopped by. You had *just* moved to LA. I was coming from a video shoot that happened to wrap early for the first time in music industry history. There were so many little things that had to line up for us to meet. It really was like so many of our experiences . . . kismet, lucky, perfect.

And I remember the second I met you, I felt completely at ease—able to exhale—I felt a sense of calmness and relief. Just the way you say "hello" translates in my brain to "You're safe with me. You don't have to overthink. I care about you." And so I'm sure everyone here would agree that whoever you're within ten feet from is guaranteed to be in a better mood because of it. It's true. And that's because every single inch of you radiates effortless warmth, light, love, safety . . . and everything about you just feels like home. You are my home.

I'll never forget us being on set recently, and at the end of the day, one of the crew members came up to you and said, "Hi, we haven't met, but I have to tell you . . . you have one of the

Figure 14.1 Scott and Mark's wedding picture. Heather Kincaid

most magical, beautiful souls of anyone I've ever been around. I couldn't leave without telling you."

First of all, let it be known that this is a normal thing that happens to Mark frequently. And then that same crew member turned to me and said, "You . . . you have got some nice jokes?"

Hmm!? But I wasn't even 1 percent offended because she was right . . . I am funny. No, no, no, it's because I was exploding with pride that I get to call you my other half, and nothing makes me happier than the fact that everyone can see and feel the special quality you have that I'm lucky enough to experience every day.

Forever now!

One of my favorite moments in our six years together . . . (and one of the million moments I fell in love with you!) . . . was when my car broke down in the middle of the street on our way to a midnight premiere of *Spider-Man*. Or as I like to call it, Spidermanio. In a moment that should've ruined our night and been very stressful, we both instead instantly made this unspoken pact to simply not be fazed by it. It was like nothing I'd ever experienced. I remember we turned to each other, and I said, "We really put the No Way Home in *Spider-Man*, huh?" and your sweet perfect laugh lit up the car. I remember it to this day. Then you literally lit up the street by turning on the headlights to act as our spotlight, you blasted one of your iconic playlists, and we danced around the car, laughed until we cried, and it was at least an hour before we remembered, "Oh shit, we should probably call triple A or something, huh?"

We were down to stay in that broken-down car forever. And that's yet another reason I'm so overwhelmed with joy to marry you. For those moments in life that get tough, for those times when things break down or don't go as planned, I know we will dance through it. I vow to make that unspoken pact with you in the harder times: to stay calm and grateful that I have the love of my life next to me to navigate anything and everything.

Marky, you really are the closest thing to magic I've ever experienced. You are magic. You are kindness. You are love. You are selfless. You are a healer . . . and you've healed every part of me. Or if not healed, made me realize the parts of me I thought were broken were actually beautifully perfect and didn't need healing. I love you more than I could ever put into words.

OK, I know this is getting long, but it's what Mark deserves, OK?!

Marky, you are the bar for what a human should be. You have set the bar Mount Everest high in every category imaginable: authenticity, optimism, calmness, presence, love. It's so powerful, and it has changed my outlook on life, love, and the world. It has changed my values. And although an impossible task, I vow to always work toward meeting you at that zero-oxygen "uh-oh where's gravity?"–level high, high bar that you've set.

I vow to always be there for you, to love you completely, and to unwaveringly care for you for the rest of time. I vow to be present, listen, and be a loving father and husband for our future family. I vow to be open, honest, logical, and solution-oriented in any argument that may arise. Fortunately, I have never been wrong about anything ever, which is kinda cool, and we can use that as our North Star . . . forever.

I promise to surprise you, amaze you, make you laugh, serenade you, and help and support you in your every endeavor or dream you can think of. And *wow*, I can't wait to dream as big as possible with you. And you know, I'll go to the ends of the earth to make any dream you have happen. You know in the movie *It's a Wonderful Life* when the guy is like, "You want the moon. I'll throw a lasso around it and I'll get you the moon"? That's going to be me for you forever.

And you know me, my toxic trait is thinking I could actually pull that off. I would literally Google "NASA employee emails"; "Can normal people go to the moon?" "Approximate cost of moon landing?" And honestly, I'm like this more than ever because of you. You make me genuinely believe that anything is possible. And now I'm unhinged, but that's on you.

You know we always talked about today being the best day of our life, and to no surprise, it has been. But the thought of spending the rest of my life with you makes me think the best is yet to come. Marky, today, I am honored to call you my other half, my confidant, my forever love. I promise to cherish you, support you, and always stand by your side.

You are everything to me, and I am the luckiest man in the world to spend the rest of my life with you. We have millions of memories already, and I am excited for the million more adventures that await us as we embark on this journey together.

Also, you look so hot. OK, I'm done.

———

Mark's vows to Scott:

Scott,

My love. This is the happiest day of my whole life. You are my best friend, my soulmate, my everything. You are without a doubt the best thing that has ever happened to me. And I still can't believe I found someone who looks at me the way that you do.

I've never met anyone quite like you before. You are so deeply kind, caring, bold, creative, and selfless. And not to mention, you are the most handsome man I have ever laid my eyes on.

You have so much love to give. Every single person you meet is instantly obsessed with you and your magnetic energy. You light up every room you're in, just by being you.

And it's no coincidence that we are getting married today on 7/7. Because today, and every day, I feel like the luckiest guy in the whole world to be loved by you.

The unconditional love you have for your family is truly so beautiful—your pure heart, thrill for life, and your unwavering optimism certainly comes from them. And I am so beyond grateful to call them my family now too. And the love you have for my parents, my siblings, nieces and nephews, makes me happier than you'll ever know.

Anyone that knows me knows that growing up, I was very, very shy, always putting pressure on myself, always so scared to stand out. But you've brought out a side to me I never knew was even possible. You've helped me to learn to love myself deeper. You've given me the strength and courage to be free. You celebrate me for every victory, no matter how big or small. You are the person who lifts me up, my biggest cheerleader, and my knight in shining armor.

I'll always remember that night in December. It was a perfect winter evening in Rockefeller Center, and you asked if I wanted to pick out engagement rings together. Little did I know just a few short months later, you would surprise me on the beach with the most beautiful proposal I could have ever imagined. I don't think I could have shook my head faster and harder than I did. It was as if time stood still. Just the two of us, as the sun set, as we promised to love each other for eternity. That moment will forever be etched in my memory and in my heart.

Scott, I love absolutely everything about you.

I love the way you hold me, the way your hand fits so perfectly in mine.

The way your sweet smile looks at me as you wake up in the morning.

The way you are so fearless, yet so logical and so thoughtful in everything you do.

I love exploring your beautiful mind, the way we can talk about our hopes and dreams together, and whole nights just feel like minutes.

I love the way you can quote the movie *Chicago* from start to finish, without missing a single word.

I love the way your face lights up when you come up with a new idea that will surely alter culture and shake the world as we know it.

I love that everywhere can be a stage for you—whether it's our living room for an audience of one, or a sold-out arena.

I love that because of you, I never feel alone.

I love that you are the best dad to both Bubba and Mozart.

And I love how big of a heart you carry, and I feel so thankful every day that that big heart loves me back.

My love, as your husband, I promise to be there every morning to tell you I love you and every night to give you a goodnight kiss.

I promise to always be your best friend, your biggest fan, and do everything I can to help you achieve your wildest dreams.

I promise to always be your date for midnight trips to frozen yogurt.

I promise to stay up until 3:00 a.m. to eagerly listen to each and every incredible new song you write, because you know that's my favorite thing.

I promise to always adventure with you side by side and talk for hours, laugh and cry.

I promise to share my whole heart with you, to dream with you, and to walk hand in hand with you through all that life brings.

I promise to always give you that extra hug when I know you need it most.

And I promise to love, cherish, and adore you the way you deserve.

Scott, I'm standing here today knowing that I have everything I'll ever need. With you next to me, I feel complete.

We can travel the whole world, but my favorite place will always be in your arms.

I truly know that I am the most loved person in the entire world, simply because I'm loved by you.

I can't wait to start a family together and begin a whole new list of memories.

I'm so completely in love with you, and I always will be.

I love you in this life and in a million more.

I love you forever.

CHAPTER 15

It's a Wonderful Life

Immediately following Scott and Mark's wedding and honeymoon in Puerto Vallarta (Punta Mita), which is the same place where Rick and I spent our honeymoon forty-plus years ago, they settled into their beautiful new home in Encino, California. The first time I saw it was when Lindsay and I went and stayed at their house for a weekend when Scott had gotten us tickets to the Grammys.

When we arrived, Scott gave us a tour of their home. Everything was large and comfortable. They had it decorated in modern creams and blacks. The swimming pool was heated almost as warm as a hot tub while their hot tub was turned into a cold plunge. Every corner was littered with dog toys, the work of their pups Bubba, Mozart, and Miles.

In the back, there was a guesthouse that Scott set up as a studio, providing a space to write and record his music. He also had a mini–photo studio in the back room, with lights and backdrops. Their wedding piano, with the well wishes from families and friends written all over it, sat in their living room. Adjacent to the piano was a shelf proudly displaying Scott's and Pentatonix's achievements. It included three Grammys, a Hollywood Walk of Fame star, YouTube awards, Streamy Awards, Shorty Awards, and the double platinum record *That's Christmas to Me* in a frame from RCA.

Other gold and platinum records, and various other accolades, were spread throughout the house and his studio, including Scott's Emmy for his coarrangement of "Ragged Old Flag." This Emmy-winning performance aired during the Super Bowl 2023. As Lindsay and I toured and marveled at their home and all of Scott's achievements, I realized Scott is halfway to an EGOT (Emmy, Grammy, Oscar, Tony) as of this writing.

Not long after the house tour, we found ourselves in their pool, enjoying the opportunity to hear about all of Scott and Mark's various upcoming plans. As I write this book, Scott is juggling a staggering total of ten projects. I wish I could share everything with you right now, but some of the details are still under wraps. I'll tell you what I can, along with the completed projects.

Ongoing and Active Projects:

- Scott is dedicated to releasing a steady stream of original songs, and he hopes to tour, when he can find the time. He has written hundreds of songs and continues to write almost daily.
- In November 2024, Scott was nominated for a Grammy for his solo song "Rose Without the Thorns" featuring Saje and Tonality. In January 2025 he was asked to open the Grammys singing "Bridge over Troubled Water."
- A musical cowritten by Scott (name to be determined) is currently in production and could be on Broadway as soon as 2025–2026.
- Scott wrote and produced the title track for the November 2024 movie *Meet Me Next Christmas* that Pentatonix starred in. The song has the same name.
- He has also written two other musicals that already have interest from big names in the industry and from television network producers.
- *How Lucky Am I*, a book written by Scott and Mark, was released on May 21, 2024, complete with a book tour. A second book called *Fa La La Family* will come out in December 2025 similar to their first book, with a Christmas and family theme.

- A movie is also in the works, but I can't give any more detail on that.
- Scott is collaborating with some big names in the industry on several TV shows.
- On top of that, Scott and Mark are promoting and managing the girl group Citizen Queen.

After talking about his current projects, my mind drifted to all the ones he's completed, both recently and long ago:

- Scott released "Parallel," a solo project, in July 2023.
- He cowrote a song with A. J. Sealy, "Heartbeat Symphony." It is the first and last song in *Luminous: Symphony of Us* that plays at Epcot Center every evening during the fireworks. Amazingly, the song is set to play every day until 2050. It began playing in December 2023.
- He has worked on Meghan Trainor's last two albums, being featured on the first one, on the song "Sensitive," and is given credit for arrangement and background vocals on four of the songs on that album. He is credited on two of the songs for writing and background vocals on her album *Timeless*, which include "Timeless" and "Forget How to Love." The song was released in June 2024. As of August, five of their songs have been streamed over a million times.
- He is featured on Loren Allred's new album, singing a duet "Come Alive" with her. They performed the song live at the GLAAD Awards and Pride Stonewall Day. The song was released in June 2024.
- Scott is featured on Jessica Vosk's November 2024 Christmas album *Sleigh* in the song "Christmas is Only Moments Away," which Scott cowrote.
- There have been countless collaborations—far too many to list them all.
- Scott has done voice acting on several shows, like *Centaurworld* and *Summer Camp Island*, and for his book, *How Lucky Am I*, and several others with PTX.

- Scott had a cameo role in *High School Music 4: The Reunion* in August 2023.
- Pentatonix appeared in the movie *Pitch Perfect 2* in 2015.
- Scott, Kirstie, and Mitch were in an episode of *Bones* in 2016, called "The Strike in the Chord."
- He has been awarded Grammys and an Emmy.

I might be missing a few, but these are the ones that come to mind.

Of course, Pentatonix keeps him busy too. We never could have guessed *how* busy when they first won *The Sing-Off,* but they have been on an exciting adventure together ever since. They have all been committed to making this work, and between their talents, chemistry, and work ethic, they are still regularly touring and making music thirteen-plus years later. They are one of the most celebrated a cappella groups in music history.

And just so fans know, PTX has an agreement: they can all do solo projects, but Pentatonix comes first.

I've had people approach me and ask how Scott manages to juggle so many projects simultaneously. Even when he was young, Scott thrived on being active. His passion for his work and his boundless creativity keep him constantly engaged. He loves what he does, and watching him in action is truly mind-blowing. Stay tuned for all his future endeavors! Every time we talk, I ask him if he is getting seven to nine hours of sleep a day, and he assures me he does. That's the mama coming out in me; I can't help myself.

Even despite his many projects, Scott and Mark cannot wait to start a family. When Scott informed me they purchased a five-bedroom home, I remarked, "Wow, five bedrooms!"

Scott explained that he and Mark wanted three or four children, so they needed a big house.

Scott said, "I loved growing up with my sisters, and we are so close as adults. I want my children to experience that same kind of close relationship in their life."

Mark, coming from a family of four children, shared this same sentiment.

I'm thrilled for Scott and Mark in their quest to start a family, and I know they will be exceptional fathers. I can't wait to welcome more grandchildren into our family, joining the five we already adore.

For decades it was a tradition in our family to watch *It's a Wonderful Life* every Christmas. OK, it was more a tradition of me making everyone watch it, but I like to think they appreciate it now. Scott, at age thirteen, even played young George Bailey in the musical, *It's a Wonderful Life*, at Theater Arlington.

The film follows the story of George Bailey, who is in a position he never wanted to be in. He is having trouble accepting himself and his lot in life. After having quite a bit of money stolen, he feels ruined, considers suicide, and wishes he'd never been born. But an angel shows George what life would be like for everyone without him, and he comes to appreciate his family and friends and sees that he has value and support. Scott's story may not be exactly the same, but the lessons resonated with him.

Scott confided in me that when he was younger and realized that he was gay, he had planned to pretend to be straight for his entire life. The fear of coming out and losing everyone he loved or never realizing his dreams tormented him. He even grappled with the question of why he had even been born.

The difference between those early years and today, with Scott fully himself, living his passion and loving his husband, reminds me of the joy and celebration at the end of that movie.

A portion of Scott's wedding vows even referenced the movie, quoting Jimmy Stewart's iconic line: "You want the moon? I'll throw a lasso around it and pull it down for you."

Maybe Scott didn't have an angel come down to help him find this gratitude and acceptance, but he did have his family and friends, his commitment to music, and the truth—that he shouldn't have to change to fit into the music industry.

Today, Scott and Mark continue to do their best to live their life to the fullest. They openly share their personal joy and creativity with the world. Their wedding, widely celebrated on social media, was met with overwhelming acceptance. Their married life is no different, as they continue to be supported and support others.

———

The pride I have in my husband, children, sons-in-law, and grandchildren continuously grows and evolves as they do. Scott and Mark are starting their family while Lauren sings in a band that keeps getting busier. Her kids are growing up—all so talented in so many ways. Lindsay is about to retire from the navy and will settle who knows where in a couple of years with her spunky, brilliant children. I watch them as they cheer each other on and support each other in everything they do, big or small. I love my family with a depth that words can scarcely describe, and I am so grateful for the life we've been blessed with. I look forward to living out our story as it unfolds, and I can't wait to see what the next chapters will bring.

It truly is a wonderful life.

Tips for Parents (and Life in General)

Here are the steps that sum up what has gotten Scott to where he is today, as I see them.

Family/Friend Support.
Scott benefited from a supportive family environment that ensured he had all the resources he needed to pursue his interests and passions. Moreover, he has always surrounded himself with incredibly talented individuals who share his deep passion for creating music and various other endeavors.

Practice Makes Perfect.
Scott had a commitment to practicing piano and singing from early morning before school and several hours after school. His dedication improved his skills and also deepened his understanding of music theory, forming a solid foundation for his creativity. In other words, learn to play an instrument. You might not become a Mozart, but it will enhance your abilities in many different ways.

Great Mentors.
Choosing the right mentors and teachers was crucial for Scott's development. It's one thing to practice, but practicing the right way (just like in sports), especially with instruments like the piano and voice, makes a big difference. Scott learned from the best, which significantly shaped his artistic path.

Collaborations.

Scott has always been incredibly sociable, making collaboration second nature to him. From childhood, he's been involved in various creative projects, such as crafting magazines with his fourth-grade friends, producing multiple albums in high school, and engaging in many collaborations with music, musicals, TikToks, and the like. He's always been eager to collaborate and explore new avenues.

This collaborative spirit led to the formation of groups like the Trio, Pentatonix, and Superfruit, as well as partnerships with prominent stars like Kelly Clarkson, Meghan Trainor, and Loren Allred, among others. (See the list in the acknowledgments.) Each endeavor has expanded his network and honed a diverse set of skills. Scott has an unstoppable commitment to creativity and loves involving his talented friends and acquaintances in many projects.

Pushing the Envelope.

Scott isn't stuck just wanting to do one thing. He constantly says yes to trying new things and getting inspired in new ways. Scott built a studio in his home during the COVID-19 pandemic and the prolonged lockdown in California. There he learned to use Pro Tools and became very good at music production, recording his original music, mixing it, and editing videos. His love of innovating and trying new things always opens up new opportunities for him.

Don't Let Fear of Failure Control You.

If you don't attempt something, you'll never have a chance at succeeding. Scott confessed that fear rarely troubled him when he was younger because he didn't dwell on things too much. However, as he entered his twenties, he found himself more prone to overthinking. It wasn't until his late twenties that Scott broke free from this habit, embracing a mindset of saying yes to every opportunity that felt right and giving his all without hesitation or fear. This was when he made the decision to start releasing original solo music again, as he did when he was younger. Whenever Scott faced rejection or disappointment, he would tell himself, *When one door closes, another one will open.* He never let a failure deter him from his goals. Instead, he would pick himself up and try even harder.

Social Media Savvy.
This became one of Scott's strengths as he grew older, making entertaining content on platforms such as YouTube, Facebook, Instagram, TikTok, Twitter (X), and even in the early days of Snapchat and Myspace. He has a great sense of what's trending and what will do well and can consistently post on social media platforms. Both Scott and Pentatonix were able to leverage social media to share their music with the world.

Networking and Socializing.
Scott has always surrounded himself with positive, creative, smart, talented people and avoided toxic people when he could. He can chat comfortably with anyone, from kids at concerts to CEOs at corporate parties. A lot of these connections he's made led him to different opportunities.

Ask, Believe, Receive.
When Scott was a teen, I read the book *The Secret* by Rhonda Byrne and shared some of what I read with him. The book is based on the idea of the law of attraction, which claims that your thoughts can influence what happens to you. The main rules are "ask, believe, receive." Now, I'm not saying that I believe everything in the book, but there is something to be said for believing your dreams can be a reality.

Fun Fact: One of the activities of the book involved creating a vision board. Scott meticulously crafted an impressive vision board when he was in his teens. He had pictures of USC, the college he wanted to attend, and of a Grammy, of which he has gotten multiple. I'm pretty sure the vision board had pictures of an Emmy (he has one), Oscar, Tony (He's on his way to an EGOT). He also had pictures from different Broadway musicals. Almost everything on that board has come to fruition.

Find Your Niche and Make It Unique.
Marty Rendleman, Scott's manager when he was sixteen to seventeen years old, once shared with me the concept of "having sizzle in the steak." She explained this meant doing something uniquely captivating that stands out and brings excitement. Scott and Pentatonix embody this idea perfectly. It's an absolute truth, particularly in the music and entertainment industry.

Passion.
Throughout Scott's life, he has emphasized that his driving force is his passion for what he does. Let your passion be your motivation. While making money is essential (you have to pay the bills), it shouldn't dominate your whole life. Most of Scott's projects stem from his genuine passion for them. I can't recall him ever mentioning money as the sole motivation. However, a lot of these projects have ended up with profitable outcomes.

Timing and Luck.
I agree with this to a point. Being in the right place at the right time can be attributed to luck. However, I am more of a believer in this quote by Zig Ziglar: "Hard work puts you where good luck can find you."

Backup Plan.
Although I wholeheartedly believed Scott would achieve his dreams, I was relieved that at USC, he had a backup plan, which I highly recommend. Breaking into this industry is challenging,

and there are many paths within the music business to explore. Consider these options as you pursue your overall dream.

———

Even though this book was primarily about Scott's musical journey, I hope the following parenting tips also came across.

- Healthy parenting involves nurturing your child's emotional, physical, and mental well-being (mind, body, soul) while providing a stable, loving home where they can thrive.
- It's important to set boundaries, offer guidance, and be present, but it's just as vital to listen and observe your child, allowing them to explore their interests and develop their personality.
- Supporting their passions and helping them navigate challenges fosters resilience and self-confidence.
- Healthy parenting requires flexibility, patience, and a deep commitment to your child's growth, encouraging them to become the best version of themselves.
- Accepting your child for who they are means embracing their individuality, strengths, and even their quirks. It involves setting aside preconceived notions or expectations and recognizing that each child is a unique individual with their own path.

Our three children pursued their own unique paths, leading Rick and me to proudly raise an artistic linguist, a singing aeronautics expert, and a musician/entertainer. This acceptance builds a strong bond between parent and child and gave my children a sense of security and self-worth. When children, straight or gay, feel accepted and loved for who they truly are, they are more likely to grow into confident, authentic adults who understand the value of self-acceptance and compassion.

Notes to Scott

From Mark, Pentatonix Members, and Others

Mark, Scott's husband

Scott, you are my rock, my whole heart, my everything. I am the luckiest person in the world to be your husband. You are the most caring, inspiring, creative, golden-hearted person I've ever known, and your love and support is something I cherish forever. I am so in awe of you and everything that you have achieved, and I know in my heart that this is just the beginning of all your wildest dreams coming true.

The fire and passion that you have for life is truly one of a kind. Watching you continuously grow, explore, and thrive as an artist, singer, songwriter, and producer makes me more proud than I can even begin to express in words. Life with you is the ultimate adventure. Late-night dance parties just us two, long car rides listening to our favorite music, deep conversations of our hopes and dreams—our list of memories together is never-ending. I love raising our pups Bubba, Mozart, and Miles together—they really are the best doggies on the planet! I hold dearly every single day we spend together as husbands, each moment tattooed on my heart for all time.

All the love and support from your mom and your entire family are such a beautiful foundation to the extraordinary person you are, and I am beyond grateful to be a part of the amazing Hoying family. Thank you to the Hoyings for welcoming me into the family with open arms and for showering Scott and me with nothing but love and warmth.

Scott, I can't wait to start a family of our own. You are going to be the most incredible father. I love you with all of my heart, forever and always!

Kirstie, Pentatonix

When I think about our friendship over the years, I think of making silly music videos and totally crushing dance videos (ha) in high school and acting out musicals on the tour bus after playing some of the greatest shows of our lives. Vastly different and actually quite similar in all the best ways, and, truly, how many friendships can endure so long and say the same? You have been a part of so many of my favorite memories, memories that have defined who I became as a person and equally memories that have just made me laugh so hard that they still bring a tear to my eye just thinking about them. We've weathered every season we've encountered in the nearly twenty years of knowing each other, and I'm very proud of the people "Scirstie" have become, and who they are on their way to being in the future.

I have always been inspired and astounded by your drive, creativity, and unabashed ambition and have always wished the absolute best for you. You are my family! You have rarely lacked in confidence for pursuing your ideas and have this uncanny ability to put your entire being behind whatever it is you believe in. This self-assurance has not only successfully gotten you to where you are but must be equally credited to Connie and Rick's supportive parenting. Any mother's, any parent's greatest wish for their child is for them to believe in themselves and their own greatness; any parent's greatest wish for themselves is to see their child flourish and to be able to be that anchor and cheerleader. Giving Scott the platform and love to succeed has touched so many lives for the better. My life has absolutely been brighter, more interesting, daring, at times more chaotic, but mostly beautifully enriched by you in it, Scott. I love you!

Mitch, Pentatonix

I can confidently say there is no one on earth like Scott. Growing up alongside him and watching him become the man he is today has been thrilling. He and I braved a lot of the scary moments of life together, and he not only arrived on the other side undeterred but with a stronger thirst for life and a deeper passion for enriching the lives of others through his art. His unrelenting ambition to pursue his dreams inspires those around him to be bold enough to follow his shining example. To know Scott is to know the true meaning of positivity, of enthusiasm, and of loving friendship.

Kevin, Pentatonix

"Scott Hoying is one of a kind" doesn't quite capture it. He's a true creative spirit, akin to the Baz Luhrmanns of the world, brimming with a million brilliant ideas at any given moment. Whether crafting a medley that spans centuries of music or perfecting every production detail of a track, he embodies boundless creativity and a relentless work ethic that pushes us all in Pentatonix to execute faster and dream bigger. Your energy and drive inspire us daily to elevate our ambitions.

And to top it off, beyond his talent, he's a genuinely kind person, a hilarious individual who doesn't take himself too seriously, and a loyal and caring friend. Thank you for being such a significant influence in my life. Because of you, I've grown immensely as a creative, and I'm a better human. I'm excited for everything that will come to you in your life.

Matt, Pentatonix

When I think of Scott, I think of someone who just loves music through to his core. We were in Vancouver after playing a show in an arena there and a friend of mine took us to a small late-night jam that happens locally. And we were both elated to check it out just to hear amazing musicians and singers. Lo and behold, they invited us up to scat/improv, and they had no idea that we were in Pentatonix but just saw the way we were reacting to the music and felt that it was infectious. So we went up there and had the absolute best time. I will always treasure that memory because I knew no matter where life takes us, Scott and I will share a deep love for music that not many can understand.

———

The following are notes that were returned on the release forms that we sent out for approval to use names and pictures in the book. They filled my heart with joy!

Keli Ferrier, Scott's first piano teacher

Scott made me work to be a better teacher. He had undeniable talent like I'd not seen before. He is the product of some amazing parenting, and I am better for having known the Hoying family. The pride I have for each of the Hoying kids is indescribable. Thank you.

Jacque Hall, elementary music teacher

I remember that he carried the musical one year. Completely carried it!! He was in second grade! I don't know of anyone else that could have!! He was why I chose it. And you, Connie, made it happen for him by availing him to every possible opportunity. I always think of you when I think of Scott. It's true!! I always think of you as well.

Laura Farnell, junior high choir teacher

I was so impressed with Scott's ability to create and understand music. One day Scott complimented specific characteristics of a choral composition I had written for their choir class to sing at a concert. First, his words demonstrated a depth of understanding about the music and its intricacies far beyond his years. Second, I was impressed that he noticed it while still in the early stages of learning the piece. The level of his emotional maturity displayed by a middle school student in articulating such discerning observations was amazing.

Another fond memory I have is when Scott sang "Mary, Did You Know?" at our church and it "brought the house down." Scott's performances always "brought the house down" on featured solos, talent show performances, and more. I loved teaching so much, and the connections I made with Scott and all of my students warm my heart to this day when I remember them. The same sincerity that makes him so endearing as a performer and person is something I've always known him to possess.

Another wonderful memory was when the students would come to the choir room before and after school so they could mess around and make music. Scott would play the piano and the kids would make up songs together, resulting in a lot of laughter and fun.

Around the time Scott moved to high school, I had our first son and stepped away from full-time teaching. I continued to play the piano at the high school where he attended and I followed his progress proudly as he excelled at Martin, made the All-State Choir, won Martin Idol and more. When I had our second son, I recorded every episode of *The Sing-Off* and remember watching Pentatonix win during a 2:00 a.m. feeding. I attended their post-*Sing-Off* performances at Martin and in Arlington, and later, PTX music became part of the soundtracks of my kids' childhood. Now my oldest is singing in Martin Chamber Singers, and he was absolutely thrilled to be a part of opening for a Pentatonix concert, which was not only a really cool full-circle moment for me but also an indication of how Scott's heart remains kind, giving, and grateful (and is a testament to all that his amazing parents poured into him.)

Kay Owens, high school choir director
Scott Hoying walked into my choir room as a ninth grader, full of energy. I knew of his talent level because I had worked with

him in a Martin High School musical production when he was in the fourth grade. We rolled through Scott's ninth grade year with him involved with every part of the choir. He auditioned for the Texas All-State choir and did not make it.

At the end of that school year, he came into my office and asked how he could make the choir. We talked about talent level and work ethic level. We talked about how those two areas have to work together. You guessed it, Scott returned in the fall of his tenth grade year with a determination and those two areas in check. I watched Scott change that year!! He made the prestigious Texas All-State Choir! He also continued that work ethic and improved his vocal skills the next two years. He became a three-year All-Stater!

As I watched Scott change and embrace the combination of his talents, work ethic, and learning to get better, I knew he was on his way to success when he left Martin High School.

And the rest is history. . . . I am so proud of this young man!

Pamela Elliott, Radio Disney Superstars and God's Country Kids director

A treasured evening at Ronald McDonald House Christmas Party was when Scott was singing "Mary, Did You Know?" and there were so many tears! We saw and heard his heart when he was singing! ♥ Another very sweet memory was one day at a Radio Disney Superstar rehearsal and Scott was giving harmony notes to the performers. He truly made their performances tremendously better! ♥ I'm so honored we got to be a part of Scott's life. So happy and proud of his talent, which is off the charts amazing, but more importantly his Heart ♥.

Stefani Little, Rhythm Nation owner and voice coach

Scott, I knew you were going to be a huge force to be reckoned with in life, even at the age of seven! I was right! Your voice and talent are amazing, but I adore your sweet, giving heart even more! You and your family have always been so very special to me, and I know where you get it from. I'm so very proud of you and all of your accomplishments; but again I'm even more proud of the kind of person you have always been. Keep being you!!!

Tom McKinney, voice coach

I met Scott Hoying when he was twelve years old and in the sixth grade. At this very young age, Scott was already showing signs of becoming a great and highly versatile artist. Scott knew that he wanted to be a broad spectrum POP artist. He was writing songs and lyrics with a mature understanding of who he was and where he wanted to go musically. He was just beginning to go through his vocal changes. Anxious about going through this vocal change and how it would affect his long-term sound and range, we began to work on vocal exercises to strengthen and expand his range and flexibility, along with proper diaphragmatic breathing, utilizing vocal projection and resonance. Always disciplined in his study, he lived and breathed his music and exceeded expectations from lesson to lesson. He proceeded to develop his own unique style and inventiveness and came through with an exceptional four-plus-octave vocal range, with flexibility, that has served him extremely well as he grew into his future role of music composer-arranger and leader of Pentatonix, the world's most successful international a cappella singing group!

As I recall, at the time we met, Scott was associated with a talent agent who was trying to push him toward country music in order to have a successful career. Country music was not Scott's interest or passion. I assured him that he should follow his interest and work on music that speaks to him. I told Scott he has freedom to become the artist-composer-performer he imagines himself to be.

It has been my honor and privilege to have worked with such a gifted talent like Scott Hoying. Bravo, Scott!

Julie Bonk, Jazz piano teacher
I remember we had such a good time writing a song together called "Coming Home." It was about a soldier coming home from war, and it was such a powerful song. I'd love to see Scott record it in time for Memorial Day. It was such a pleasure teaching Scott all those years. I'm so incredibly proud of him.

Glen Pace, producer, recording engineer, and owner of Starplex Records
When I was judging the talent show at Johnnie High's Music Review, I was floored when Scott, a twelve-year-old, got up and started singing "Bridge over Troubled Water." I quickly realized this contest was over as he had four standing ovations in the first half of the song. What a Talent!!

Big Phazz, songwriter, recording engineer, producer
Collaboration with Scott has consistently been an incredible experience. We've shared some remarkable recording sessions, including the inclusion of my song, "Hey Kim," on his 2008 self-titled album, *SCOTT HOYING*. Another memorable moment arose when my son Bryce Clark's middle school principal, Jerry R. Burkett, discovered my background as a music producer with my own studio. Upon learning this, he presented me with a song he had penned titled "If I Could My Way," seeking a vocalist. Instantly Scott came to mind, especially since we had recently collaborated on a project with Kidd Kraddick from 106.1 KISS FM and record producer Robi Menace. I reached out to Scott, who graciously agreed to participate. In April 2010, he visited my home studio in Grand Prairie, Texas. Jerry provided Scott with the lyrics and melody, while Jerry and I collaborated on composing the music. Once the composition was finalized, I was ready to engineer and record his vocals. Scott entered the booth and delivered a masterful performance that left us in awe of his talent. It was evident to both of us that he was destined for superstardom.

Robi Menace, producer

Kidd Kraddick told me about this six-foot-plus, fifteen-year-old kid with blond hair and freckles that could sing like a bird. I didn't believe him but I said let's try it and we cut some songs. And we recorded Kidd's Kids song for the annual charity, and I watched Scott over the years develop into something really special!!! Kidd and I always knew he had "it," and he showed the world we were right!

Marty Rendleman, manager

I'll never forget when we went to California and met with Seth Riggs. He asked Scott to play and sing a song on the piano. He decided to sing "Georgia on my Mind." When he finished, Seth told him that Ray Charles played that same song on that very same piano and stated how impressed he was by Scott's rendition. I'll never forget the look on Scott's face! I knew Scott was something special. I'm so proud of all you've accomplished, Scott.

Caleb Cameron, producer, songwriter, and manager

I have a really fun memory from our time in Nashville. We put together a band of supertalented young musicians to create the production for Scott's EP *Currently Single*. We spent an entire day in the basement of someone's house rehearsing the songs and coming up with all the production ideas. After a few hours, things really started to gel and everybody in the room knew we had something great happening. We were having a blast making music and listening to this great band be great.

I remember Rick was having such a fun time seeing it all come together. Except for Rick and Scott, we were all college students, so of course, we were broke. LOL. After like five hours, Rick said, "Are you guys hungry?" We were like, "Yes!" Rick went and picked up pizzas and beer for everybody. We couldn't believe it! It was the best day ever. We were making an album in

Nashville, eating pizza, and drinking beer. Surely this had to be just how it was with all the legends of music who came before us.

Now my memory is a little hazy on whether or not Rick let fourteen-year-old Scott have a drink with us. That sounds like something only the coolest dad would do. If you've ever seen Rick on a motorcycle, that should tell you all you need to know about that. ;) Now as a dad myself all these years later, I can't help but think about what an amazing moment and memory that Rick was intentional to make with his son. I look for those special moments myself, hoping to grab them whenever they appear just like a hot slice of pepperoni and a cold one.

RJ Knapp, songwriter, producer, manager
When I think about the brief time Caleb Cameron and I spent with Scott, there are two things that stick out to me. First, at the time at least, he had a ritual of eating a bowl of Wendy's chili before every recording session. I've never met any musician with a vocal preparation ritual so unique before or since! But hey, the stuff that was coming out of that guy's vocal cords was just nuts! Second, and more importantly, it was amazing to watch Scott work, even as a young high schooler. At fourteen years old, he was able to not only keep up with trained, professional vocalists almost a decade older than him at Belmont University, one of the premier commercial music universities in the country, but he pushed the envelope and inspired everyone on the project to excel. Yet even with all his talent, he was humble, eager, and adventurous. It was obvious he was touched with a special gift and was on a path to do amazing things musically. His worldwide success doesn't surprise me at all.

Josh Goode, producer, songwriter, arranger, mixer
Scott was absolutely the best vocalist I have ever worked with in the studio, and I have worked with some incredibly talented artists. One of my favorite memories was when we were working

on the bridge for "Waiting," a song we had recently written together. Bradley (a recording engineer) and I asked him to try a vocal riff toward the end of the bridge, which was headed into a new key. When Scott sang it, we were blown away . . . but what was even more amazing was that after he harmonized over that riff, he then built an entirely new background vocal melody (which he also harmonized and stacked over his melody multiple times). We then had the entire back half of the piece filled up with soaring vocals, sounding like a massive choir in about thirty minutes.

I will never forget his prodigal prowess in the studio, but I will also always remember how hilariously bored he seemed in the studio at the time. Here was this seventeen-year-old kid just scorching us with takes and walking away with the attitude of *What? Is there anything else you need?* as we scrambled to catch up!! LOL. . . .

What I love most about Scott, however, is not his extreme vocal talent. I would bet that the real reason everyone loves him is his warmth, grace, and humility as a person and as a singer. He is never "too famous" for friends or family and is a very well-grounded, wonderful person whom I could not be happier for.

David Lambert, actor, voice recorder, producer
I met Scott at a monthly artist networking event called "Exposure Showcase" around 2007–2008, where actors and singers would perform in front of a panel of judges consisting of agents, casting directors, and other industry professionals. Scott was singing one of his original songs. I had just opened a small recording studio where I primarily recorded voice-overs and knew nothing about producing music but wanted to learn and needed to practice on someone. I approached Scott and asked if he would come to my studio and play around with some songs for free. He was still in high school, but he was so meticulous about what he wanted and knew how to get it. I knew I wasn't just dealing with some

kid tinkering around with a keyboard. He was an artist with the skills of a veteran musician. We recorded about eight to ten songs (mostly work of his). My wife at the time threatened me with divorce if I ever charged him a penny.

Chris Sampson, vice dean of Thornton Music School at USC
I have very fond memories of watching Ben Bram (who was studying with me at the time) connect with Scott and watch them develop and grow together. I also remember Scott updating me as the group progressed through *The Sing-Off* as (I believe) he still had one eye on the possibility of returning to school.

Ben Bram, arranger, recording engineer, producer
Where do I begin, haha!!! After thirteen years of memories, it's so difficult to zero in on anything specific, but I will say this: Working with Scott has been one of the great joys of my life. Finding someone so aligned, driven, talented, and optimistic to create with is incredibly rare, and I feel so lucky to have crossed paths with him.

Genevieve Lamb, hair and makeup artist
Scott has a unique way of making you feel truly valued. When you become friends with Scott, you gain a friend for life. There's something special about him that lights you up whenever you see him. Whether he's onstage or in a makeup chair, he makes everyone around him feel special, and you always get the genuine Scott. He gives his all and is fully present when he's with you. I feel so lucky to have him in my life.

Candice McAndrews, stylist
I love you, Scott. Watching you grow and become the man you are today has been such a gift. I am honored to call you my friend and family. I love you so much!

Ryan Parma, director, videographer

I think some of my fondest memories of Scott boil down to one characteristic: an everlasting sense of adventure and enthusiasm. When I was traveling with Pentatonix back in 2014, Scott would always be up for day adventures. I would plan for the group during our off time on tour, even if he would be the only member that came out—whether that be taking a trek up the arch of St. Louis or exploring the city of London. And to this day, each and every interaction I have with Scott leaves me more motivated and inspired to just go for what I want and dream big. He is the living embodiment of believing with your whole being to pursue your passions and the world will work itself out. His support and continued friendship means the world to me, and I am so blessed to know him.

Jake Updegraff, social media

One of my favorite memories of Scott is how thoughtful he is. I could list so many things like throwing me the most epic birthday weekend in Las Vegas for my twenty-fifth or giving me his nice clothes that he could easily sell and make a profit. But what I remember most is when he got me a video of one of my favorite celebrities growing up. It was from David Archuleta, and Scott knew how much of a fan I was. David was backstage at a PTX show and while there, Scott filmed him with the band with David saying a nice gesture to me, giving me a shoutout. It's probably silly, but to me I remember being on cloud nine— not only because I got a video from someone I was a fan of since my teens, but because Scott thought of me in that moment. I didn't ask him for that, nor did he gain anything from it. He just did it from the kindness of his heart because that's who Scott is: a kind and thoughtful human being. He gives as much as loves . . . so when he loves you, you're gonna know it.

Alexis Lowes, tour manager

I have been touring for over twenty-five years and have worked with some of the biggest names in the business, and I can say without hesitation working with Scott and Pentatonix have been some of my very favorite tours of my life. Scott is talented, funny, kind, and he would never let me forget to say handsome. His talent is immense and only matched by the joy and bright light he brings to all around him. Love you, Scott, always.

Sarah Crossland, assistant tour manager

Scott, I'll never forget the moment I first met you. It was a Halloween party, you were a giraffe and I was Amy Winehouse, of course. I had no idea playing party games in the backyard then that seven years later, I'd come to consider that giant giraffe man as one of the most special people in my life. There's a million things to love about you, but I have to say, truly, I've never met someone with the ability to be as endlessly creative as you. Whether you're writing a song, book, choreographing a new dance, or creating your next tour TikTok, the creative energy you embody is unmatched. The only thing that shines brighter than your creativeness is your unending love for your people. Whether it be your amazing husband, friends, family, or fans, it's hard to find someone who cares more deeply or is more passionate about making sure that the people around you are seen and taken care of. I've seen you showcase it in so many ways, so many times . . . some so far under the radar nobody would ever know but the person on the receiving end of your generous heart. The confidence you have in who you are and how you share that with the world is something I admire so much. You make everyone who encounters you somehow feel less alone simply by being authentically you, and that is such an incredible gift. I could go on for days, this we know, but I'll end now by saying quite simply that I adore you, and I am so so proud of the human you are. I love you, Scotty!

Lindsey B, choreographer

I love Scott's fearlessness and dedication to creativity. Creating with him is one of my greatest joys.

Mario Jose, assistant manager (early years)

Whew. That's a good "whew"—like a sigh of relief knowing I've had a friend like you "whew." I look back on our ten-plus-year friendship and I smile, I tear up, and I thank my lucky stars that we crossed paths. I know people warned us about LA—"Be careful, LA is full of phonies"—but we have had an unbreakable, genuine bond from moment one. I have never had a friend that has been in my corner as much as you have. You believe in me like family does, and I hope you know I believe in you just the same. From Spaulding Sessions, to late-night heart-to-hearts on the tour bus, to wild nights out in random cities, to sessions belting out Katy Perry covers, to sharing the stage with you in front of thousands of people—*you are family to me.* It doesn't matter how long we go without seeing each other, I know the moment we reunite, it's like a day hasn't passed, and we belly laugh all night long. We have seen each other come from young, hungry kids to seasoned vets that have toured the world! We've gone from broke, struggling music college students to educated, Grammy Award–winning musicians who are domestic dog dads! Seeing you marry Mark, the love of your life, made me so happy because you both deserve the world and the world is yours to take. You have been the best boss, the best musical peer, the best karaoke partner, and best friend to me since day one, and I am so happy we get to share a lifetime of friendship together. Cheers to the next ten years and beyond! I love you so much! With a song in my heart.

Ken Phillips, publicist

I knew from that very first time I met the group at their apartment(s) near The Grove that Scott was a leader. He had the most questions for me in that first meeting and had an aura of greatness about him.

I could tell he was a standout and had that hunger to conquer the world that I look for when taking on new clients.

Acknowledgments (It Takes a Village)

Thank you so much to every individual mentioned in this book. You believed in Scott's potential, giving him the confidence to pursue his dreams. Your kindness and support made all the difference. Every one of you brought unique perspectives, experiences, and skills that shaped Scott professionally and individually. Thank you for making an impact on Scott and being integral parts of his life and growth. He is who he is because of everyone who took the time for him. It truly takes a village, and we are privileged to have known you all.

Every one of these talented people had a part in Scott's growth in one way or another.

K–High School
Kidd Kraddick
Johnnie High
Jacque Hall
Laura Farnell
Kay Owens
Marlene Bigley
Pamela Elliott
Stefani Little
Tom McKinney
Colleen McKinney
Keli Ferrier
Julie Bonk

Josh Rodgers

Steve Huisman Mark

Glen Pace

JoDee Payne

Caleb Cameron

RJ Knapp

JoJo Davis

Josh Goode

Bradley Prakope

Big Phazz

Robi Menace

David Lambert

Marty Rendleman

All the bands involved in Scott's projects or shows

After High School

Pentatonix

Pentatonix crew

Chris Sampson

Ben Bram

Ed Boyer

Grant Cornish

Bill Hare

Dr. Bill Dorfman

MaryCatherine Finney

Ken Phillips

Ryan Parma

Jake Updegraff

Candice McAndrews

Thomas McAndrews
Lindsey Blaufarb
Craig Hollamon
Genevieve Lamb
Sarah Baczewski
Alexis Lowes
Sarah Crossland
Mario Jose
Grady Brown
Michiko Dixit
Jason Bennet
Austin McGuire
Ben Hausdorff
Citizen Queen
Esther Koop
Nichole Faulkner
Kate Bella
Pretty Sister

Collaborators
Meghan Trainor
Kelly Clarkson
Jennifer Hudson
Tori Kelly
Loren Allred
Dolly Parton
Andrea Bocelli
Lindsey Stirling
Jessica Vosk

Andy Grammer
Amber Lu
Säje & Tonality
Jason Derulo
Cost n' Mayor
Rozzi Crane
Kina Grannis
Betty Who
Hillary Duff
Maren Morris
Randy Jackson
A Girl Named Tom
Diane Warren
Ringo Starr
Jazmine Sullivan
Frankie Bird
David Archuleta
Martin Johnson
Shams Ahmed
Joey Orton
Brad Silnutzer
A. J. Sealy
Petro AP
Toby Gad, cowriter of "Pray"
Angelina Jordan
Pentaholics: the best fans on the planet!

This Book
My family
Michael Tan
Lily Hirsch
Ken Phillips
Molly Frisinger

Photographers
Ben Hausdorff, cover
Lindsay Hoying Fondren, engagement photos
Heather Kincaid, wedding pictures
Jamie Haswell, author and publicity pictures
Paul Knudsen, musical pictures
Josh Adams, Johnnie High pictures
Luke Fontana, Superfruit picture

I know there are people I forgot. I am so sorry, and if it makes you feel better, know that it will probably haunt me for the rest of my life.

To My Family

Scott,

Thank you for making our family's life so endlessly fascinating. You have taken us on unforgettable adventures worldwide, providing countless memories (and material for this book). Your ideas and enthusiasm have been so contagious, often sparking ideas or memories that evolved into entire chapters.

I'm so proud of the man you've become; your compassion, kindness, and generosity shine through in everything you do. You inspire those around you with your authenticity and belief in the impossible. You are an incredible combination of hard work and talent. Thank you for inspiring me to bring this book to life.

Lindsay,

Your support has been the backbone of this project. You spent countless hours reviewing, refining, and reorganizing. You understood my voice and helped make this something I'm proud of. We spoke almost daily for months, brainstorming and collaborating. It's been such a joy to have this time with you.

Your help with the technical "computer stuff" allowed me to focus on remembering the last thirty-plus years and writing without distraction. Your organizational skills and random FaceTimes to walk me through Google Drive are the only reasons I could keep everything straight.

Above all, your encouragement helped me believe in myself and this project. Whenever I felt unsure or like I was fooling myself, your insistence on the project's potential kept me going through to completion. Believing in the impossible runs in the family, I guess.

Lauren,

Your memories of this time, insightful critiques, and brilliant ideas were indispensable. I know you are impossibly busy with a demanding job, singing in a band, and two very active boys, yet you still made time for me and this dream of mine. I don't know how you managed that, but it meant the world to me, and your honest feedback and suggestions helped shape this book.

I also want to thank you and Robbie for celebrating every milestone along this journey—finishing the book, publisher interest, publisher offer, contract signed, and so forth. With every new piece of news about the book, big or small, you made me feel like a star. These celebrations meant so much to me. Thank you from the bottom of my heart.

Rick,

My soulmate and partner, I love you. Your support and small acts of kindness have been appreciated. Whether bringing me coffee or working through rough spots in the book with me, you always believed in me, and I don't know what I'd do without you.

Through countless late nights, moments of doubt, and bursts of inspiration, you stood by me, never complaining, and helped me with whatever I needed. I appreciate your wisdom, the creative way you see the world, and your steady presence. You have been my rock for more than forty years of marriage, and I'm looking forward to forty more years (it could happen; science has come a long way, and I've had pretty good luck believing in the impossible).

INDEX

About the Author

Connie Hoying lives in Fort Worth, Texas, with her supportive husband and soulmate, Rick. She is a devoted mom and grandmother, retired physical therapist, and now a published author. Throughout her life, she has raised three incredibly successful children whose careers have taken her and her husband around the world. In her retired years, she finds joy in spoiling her five grandchildren, traveling, and writing. Frequently approached by parents seeking advice on raising successful children, particularly regarding her son Scott's achievements in the challenging entertainment industry, Connie was inspired to share her experiences in this book.

.